Praise for *Get Over "I Got It"*

"As a superwoman-in-recovery myself, *Get Over "I Got It"* was the book I needed all along. Elayne lays out a simple step-by-step pathway to discover how to ask for what you want, avoid burnout, and understand the value of surrounding yourself with a network of supportive women"
—**Kelly Notaras, CEO of KN Literary Arts and Author of *The Book You Were Born to Write***

"Elayne Fluker is the real deal and truly a force of nature, and this raw and insightful book is a complete game changer every goal-oriented woman should read at least once."
—**Maya Penn, Award-winning CEO and Eco-Entrepreneur**

"This is the book I've been waiting for. Elayne Fluker taps into the core essence of female power to not only unlock our potential but to also know that we don't have to do it all alone. A must-read for women starting out or well within their career."
—**Stephanie Nadi Olson, Founder of We Are Rosie**

"Elayne inspires twenty-first-century 'superwomen' in a new way, encouraging us to recognize that asking for, enlisting, and accepting support is one of the keys to living a life that is full."
—**Tai Beauchamp, Serial Entrepreneur and Cofounder of Brown Girl Jane**

"Elayne lights the way with her wisdom-filled stories, encouragement, directives, and interviews with professionals. Read this book—and learn from the best!"
—**Dr. Zoe Shaw, Psychotherapist and Author of *A Year of Self-Care***

"Elayne Fluker has hit the mark in *Get Over "I Got It"* by showing the strength of being vulnerable and calling in the support you require."
—**Barbara Biziou, Transformational Vision Coach and Author of *The Joy of Ritual***

"Reading *Get Over "I Got It"* is like having a friend in your head who is there to remind you that even greater things are possible when you are in it together! Elayne's book has my heartfelt recommendation!"

—Tyrona Heath, Director of Market Engagement for The B2B Institute at LinkedIn

"This book is written in the language that we, as unapologetically ambitious women, understand, and forces you to do the uncomfortable work necessary to be and, more importantly, *feel* successful."

—Polina Hanin, Principal at Aequitas Partners

"We're all so tired and burned out by the old school mindset of 'hustle harder.' Elayne nails the concept that rest and support is a source of strength, not weakness. A must-read for women of all ages and life stages."

—Martine Resnick, Cofounder of The Lola

"Elayne peels back the layers and goes deep by sharing her personal experience, as well as those of other influential women who've benefited from seeking support, establishing boundaries, and taking off their capes to prioritize themselves."

—Nadia Lopez, Educator and Founder of Mott Hall Bridges Academy

"As a recovering 'I got it' addict, I greatly appreciate Elayne's perspective and challenge to step away from constantly trying to prove ourselves and to step into relationship, connection, and support—a necessary shift for women in order to live a healthy life."

—Carissa Reiniger, CEO of Silver Lining

GET OVER

"I Got It"

HOW TO STOP PLAYING SUPERWOMAN,
GET SUPPORT, AND REMEMBER THAT HAVING
IT ALL DOESN'T MEAN DOING IT ALL ALONE

ELAYNE FLUKER

CREATOR OF THE *SUPPORT IS SEXY* PODCAST

HARPERCOLLINS
LEADERSHIP

AN IMPRINT OF HARPERCOLLINS

Published by HarperCollins Leadership, an imprint of HarperCollins Focus LLC.

Any internet addresses, phone numbers, or company or product information printed in this book are offered as a resource and are not intended in any way to be or to imply an endorsement by HarperCollins Leadership, nor does HarperCollins Leadership vouch for the existence, content, or services of these sites, phone numbers, companies, or products beyond the life of this book.

ISBN 978-1-4002-1380-1 (eBook)
ISBN 978-1-4002-1379-5 (PBK)

Library of Congress Control Number: 2021930827

Printed in the United States of America
21 22 23 LSC 10 9 8 7 6 5 4 3 2 1

For Annie B. and Luke

CONTENTS

CONTENTS

INTRODUCTION

I know you've got it going on. I know, to everyone else, you appear as though you're unstoppable, like you need no one, like you have it all together. You're a boss chick. You're a leader. You run things. You're the one people bet on when they need something done, and they need it done right. And you take great pride in knowing that, for them, betting on you is a freakin' safe bet. You show up. You come all the way through. You do whatever it takes.

And whenever anyone has the gall to ask if you could use their help, your first response, without even thinking is, "I got it!" With a little attitude even, maybe a defiant hand held up that says "Halt!" and stops them in their tracks. Because, help? Why would you need their help? You're Superwoman, right? Superwoman doesn't need anyone's help.

Here's the thing, though, my sister in ambition: Superwoman. Isn't. Real. Okay? She is a fantasy, and your flawed pursuit of that perfection doesn't make you an admirable hero. More likely it leaves you feeling isolated, unsupported, stressed, and unhappy. Because what every super woman *really* needs is support, whether she admits it or not.

So, it's time. It's time for you to get over what I call "I Got It!" Syndrome and learn how to truly accept support into your life. When you say the words, "I got it!" it may lead you to feel strong and accomplished in the moment, but in actuality, you're pausing all the possibilities and support that could come your way, and doing that actually keeps you small. "I got it!" cuts support off at the pass. It tells the Universe to keep it movin', when all it ever wants to do is show up for you.

And besides, even if you do have it when you say, "I got it!" do you really *have* to get it each and every single time? Do you have to carry all the groceries to the car by yourself? Or can the guy who works there, who is supposed to help you, give you a hand?

Do you have to take the kids to every single after-school activity? Or can you coordinate with another parent so you split the responsibilities of getting them where they need to be?

Do you have to work on that big project at the office by yourself into the wee hours of the morning, to the point where your body is trembling with exhaustion? Or can you accept the support of a colleague you trust and make this a team effort?

If you find yourself shaking your head side to side and saying, "Yeah . . . no, I really got this," as you read this, I understand. You might not see support even if the word were stamped backward on your forehead and you were gazing at yourself in the mirror. Again, I understand. I understand, because I've been you. I've been the woman who wants to have it all *and* do it all—at work, at home, in relationships, and every-where else. I've stood tall as the one who could shoulder the world, even if I could feel it weighing me down, or who fumbled through an opportunity just to prove to myself that I could do it by myself. In each case where my stubbornness and insecurities caused me to shun support, accepting that support would have made me stronger and wiser, and it would have taken me much further.

You may not realize this, but you deserve support. Do hear me? You, yes, *you*, reading this introduction right now. There's a reason you're reading this page, right now, in this moment. You need to hear this. You, the woman who has it all together and struts down the street or through the office or at that networking event or in pictures on the 'gram like she needs no one (or struggles to at least appear that way). *You* deserve support. And shifting your mindset around support, seeking it out and welcoming it into your space as your true superpower will change your life, advance your career, strengthen your relationships, and open you up to more fulfillment, peace, and success than you can imagine.

Right now, you're the woman who does it all. I know. And as I said, you take pride in that. Whether it's handling your business or taking care of your family, you'd rather "get it" yourself, because you don't think anyone else is as capable. But I also know there's probably a part of you that really doesn't want to, if you're honest. Not all the time. Maybe you keep things going, but most times you feel exhausted. Maybe there are other things you want to do with your time or energy, but you're busy putting everyone else first. Maybe you feel like you're the only one who can handle things at the office or at home, so you cut out what really matters to you to have more time to save the world. Or maybe you're just protecting this perfect image you've created of the woman who can do it all. You have moments when you wonder why people don't show up for you, why you're the only one who shows up for everyone else, yet you push those thoughts to the side and keep busy tackling your ever-growing to-do list on your own.

But trust me: you do not have to do this alone. Stop stressing and struggling, and choose support. It's a choice between life and *waaay* too much stress—stress that can potentially affect more than your happiness, your relationships, your business, or your climb up that career ladder. Stress can lead to serious issues with your health, and in the worst cases, it can be deadly.

I know that's heavy to drop in a career and personal development book, but you need to know this. Let's get real about it, because I'm really serious about warning successful, ambitious, go-getter women like you about the dangers of not getting support, and I will encourage you to do so by any means necessary. We get constant reminders every single day of just how necessary this is, whether it's stories of women we know personally or women we admire. But somehow, most of us still manage to ignore it. That ends today, sis!

One sobering reminder for me about the importance of this mindset shift around support was the suicide of beloved fashion designer Kate Spade. I was at my parents' home in Atlanta when I first heard the tragic news. I didn't know Kate Spade personally and have never worked with her or her company, but the news rocked my world.

Suicide? Kate Spade, whose designs brought so much joy to so many people around the world? Kate Spade, whose chipper voice and seemingly easygoing spirit I listened to on the *How I Built This* podcast when she appeared with her husband and business partner and shared the incredible story of the creation and evolution of her business? Kate Spade, who sold her business for millions and was seemingly so . . . successful? This is in no way a judgment of her. I know nothing about Kate Spade's real life. I respect her and her legacy greatly, and my heart goes out to her family. It just seemed unfair that a woman who had blessed so many with such delight was evidently in so much pain.

In the days following her death, Kate's husband, Andy Spade, told the *New York Times* that the designer had suffered from depression and anxiety for many years and was receiving support from her doctors. They were in touch with her the evening prior to her death and there was no indication, he shared, that she intended to end her life that day.[1]

I am not naive here. I know that success, money, fame, and other accolades are not enough to heal feelings of depression or isolation for us as women. Remarkably, despite the undeniable progress for women over the years, suicide rates for women ages forty-five to sixty-four rose 63 percent since 1999, according to the Centers for Disease Control and Prevention,[2] making these women the age group with the second largest percentage increase of suicides over the past two decades. (The group with the largest increase? Girls ages ten to fourteen.)

I know that, sometimes, the glowing items that make us look great on paper and make our lives look enviable on social media can add more pressure than respite. I also know what it's like to hide your depression and your feelings for fear that it will tarnish your image—whether you have a public persona or not. And I know how isolated I felt when I, someone who was always praised as the "good girl," who had it all together and was spoiled with all the "things" she wanted throughout her childhood, attempted suicide as a teenager by swallowing a handful of pills and ended up in the hospital.

See, depression has been a part of my life for many years, long before I even knew what to call it, how to recognize it, how to understand it, and how to admit that it existed as a part of me. I just knew that I had what I call "dips" occasionally—some deeper than others. I would feel a literal dip in my mood or demeanor. I continue to learn new tools and techniques to manage these dips as an adult, especially since—as an entrepreneur—the emotional ups and downs for many of us commonly happen within the same doggone day, and the occasional disappointments can be crushing. Daily meditation, daily exercise, healthy eating, and healthy habits all help. As did, recently for me, medication, which I'll share more about in a later chapter.

And the most indispensable tool that now sits atop all the others in my toolbox?

Support.

Getting support for myself in whatever ways that looks like, without judging myself for needing it, and knowing without a doubt that I deserve it, has been a game changer for me. It relieved unnecessary stress, it helped me see new possibilities in my life, it connected me to people who aligned with my vision, it opened up new opportunities for me in my career and my business, and it helped me grow as a human being.

But it wasn't until I was in my forties that I learned just how imperative it is to ask for support and to accept it, no matter how accomplished I am on paper or anywhere else. Until then, I thought I was an ambitious, successful, independent woman who was doing just fine all by herself, thank you very much.

And that's what this book is about. Reminding you, a successful, unapologetically ambitious woman who likely has the great career or the booming business or the adorable family or the amazing girlfriends—or all of the above—that you, too, must learn how to ask for and accept support and get over "I Got It!"

I recognize this may be a big shift for you as a woman who lives by the get-stuff-done code. After all, I, too, have always viewed asking for support as a sign of weakness and neediness, and I have been unconsciously telling myself that same story my whole life.

I come from a family of super-strong supporters, people who give, give, give, and then give some more; yet ask for nothing—ever—in return. My parents, the most generous people I know in this world, are the rocks within our family and true givers from the heart. They take great pride in stepping up to handle business (even when that business ain't necessarily theirs to handle).

Time after time, as I was growing up in our small-but-charming home in Long Island, New York, I witnessed my folks welcoming people in and supporting whomever needed help within our family, and within our community, in different ways. And usually those times were during some crisis for the person(s) receiving the support: abuse, abandonment, divorce, addiction, illness, financial stress, and so on. You know: life.

But even though they were, and still are, kind, loving, and happy to give, my parents struggled in their own times of need to ask for and accept support for themselves. As I write this book, both are now in their nineties, yet to this day, they say they don't want to feel they're "bothering anybody." Even if they're going to a doctor's appointment, for example—a professional who is supposed to help and support them and who is trained to do so—I often have to push them to share what's really wrong, what they're experiencing, what hurts, and what their needs are.

So, as an extremely sensitive, quiet, pensive, and observant child, I adopted the belief early on that support is best given, not received. To give meant you were noble; to receive meant that you were in the midst of some sort of crisis. People who have it all together don't need support, right?

For many of us unapologetically ambitious women today—women who are encouraged at every turn to declare ourselves as "badasses" just to prove how strong, competent, "flawless," and fearless we are—this same, dangerous belief about support is often present, and it manifests as "I Got It!" Syndrome. We have these self-inflicted expectations to "have it all," and keep it all together, all the time, all by ourselves. And the idea of allowing ourselves to be vulnerable, open, soft, and human is often terrifying because we imagine it will make us appear weak. As a result, we wear the mask, walk alone, and often carry heavier burdens than we need to. Meanwhile, our dreams, our lives, our careers, our relationships, and our health suffer the consequences.

This revelation didn't truly take shape for me until early 2015. I was craving something more in my life, although I didn't know exactly what that "more" was. I did know that there was more that I could contribute to the world, and there were more experiences waiting for me.

But there was a blockage, something that kept me from moving forward. Fear? I didn't know. But I was at a point in my life when I felt like I should be happy and fulfilled. Instead, I was just searching.

I had enjoyed a great career in media for nineteen years as a writer, editor, and content creator at some of the industry's top media outlets, including *Martha Stewart Living*, *People*, *HuffPost*, and *Essence*. I had appeared as a featured guest on the *TODAY* show, *Nightline*, CNN, HLN, VH1, BET, Sirius XM Radio, and many more, and I had spoken on stages at the United Nations, the Essence Festival, New York University, Spelman College, Howard University, and Columbia University. I love creating content for women. And in 2012, fed up with the omission of diverse images and experiences of women of color in the media, I decided to start my own media company, ChicRebellion.TV—an online video network empowering women of color to control their own narratives and share their stories. The network featured videos from women of color around the world, and launched with four original web series—which I executive-produced, casted, and financed by myself. One series was fashion, one was food, one was lifestyle, and one was for moms. (In my head, I was the Bravo for women of color—although I definitely didn't have the Bravo budget. I'm ambitious, remember?)

After two years of moonlighting, I decided, in October 2014, to quit my then-full-time, high-level, six-figure-a-year, salaried, editorial job at *Martha Stewart Living* to commit to my own company full-time—with no real plan, mind you. Come 2015, ChicRebellion.TV was experiencing great buzz but slow-to-no growth in revenue. I was still carrying all of the financial weight on my own, and that load was quickly getting hella heavy. I didn't have the money to produce more videos the way that I wanted to. I felt stuck and as though I had failed. I knew nothing about running a business and it showed. Plus, I didn't know how to ask for support.

Just before my forty-second birthday in February, those what-the-heck-am-I-doing-with-my-life questions started to bubble to the surface. I again felt alone, because in many ways I, again, *was* alone: I was single, no hubby, no kids, no business partner even—although I absolutely had plenty of love in my life thanks to a solid group of sister-friends spread across the country and my dear parents. Still, I was searching, I was stuck, I was struggling, I was low, and though I was consulting with several different brands to bring money in, my bills—without that regular, six-figure salary in a relentlessly expensive New York City—were quickly piling up.

While brunching (and on the verge of boo-hooing) one morning in Brooklyn, a couple of my close friends and former colleagues—Janel Martinez and Suncear Scretchen told me about a workshop called Momentum Education that they thought could help me find myself and my way. Because of confidentiality and respect for the process of the program, they didn't tell me many details about it, but each swore by it. Even though their secrecy seemed cryptic and kind of weird, I trusted them, and after attending an introductory gathering for Momentum, I signed up. That experience forever changed my life.

I began my journey with Momentum during the weekend of Valentine's Day in 2015, just before my birthday, and continued through the summer. It was in the leadership portion that summer that my broken relationship with support (and the restraints that this broken relationship put on my personal life, my business, and my dreams) really became apparent to me.

In a group of about forty individuals—all powerful leaders from diverse backgrounds, industries, accomplishments, and life experiences—there were two things that seemed very difficult for most of us to request when pushed to do so: 1) love and 2) support. And when I say "difficult," I'm talking about snotty-nose, ugly-crying, distraught, can hardly speak difficult. The struggle was real.

Why? Because expressing the desire or need for both love and support requires a level of vulnerability and transparency most of us have become masters at concealing in order to show up as "strong" and "successful" in our worlds, in whatever way we each defined those attributes. "I got it!" was our go-to, baby! Inside, however, many of us were hurting and craving connection. We had been choosing, unnecessarily, to wear the mask and walk alone, not realizing how much further we could go, how much more we could accomplish, how many more people we could impact, and how much fuller our lives would be if we allowed people to show up for us.

Again and again, during my time in Momentum, I witnessed firsthand the power of support, of vulnerability, of transparency, of accountability, and of having a community of powerful, like-minded individuals rally around me and around my goals for my business and, most important, for my life. The results of rewiring my beliefs and reframing my relationship with support were tangible and all-around transformative—it opened me up to opportunities and experiences I may have otherwise missed, and it relieved the loneliness and isolation I was experiencing. Sometimes the support came in whispers, sometimes in whirlwinds, sometimes it was serendipitous, sometimes it was strategic. Each time, it was what I needed in the moment. I realized: I deserve support, and it was available to me in abundance.

That experience triggered a complete mindset shift for me, one that opened my eyes to this notion that support wasn't something to avoid, it was something to embrace in whatever way I needed to, and the way I needed to was to see it as sexy. Because, tell the truth: Who doesn't want to get closer to something sexy?! Think about your last sexy vacation, a sexy home you've visited, that sexy outfit that you love to put on whether you're just dancing around in front of your mirror or going out with your girls. They make you smile, right?

Following my experience with Momentum, as I went back to my everyday life and worked hard to figure out my business, I constantly reminded myself that support is sexy (a phrase I adopted as my personal mantra and used as a hashtag on social media—#supportissexy). I pushed myself, no matter how uncomfortable at first, to make the connections I needed to lift me up. It's easy to accept something in theory, but much more of a challenge to make it a practice—and I needed a lot of practice.

Eventually, I began to notice how many other women like me—whether entrepreneurs, career women, or caregivers handling their business and "making it happen"—were unwittingly choosing to struggle alone because they didn't want to risk the shame of asking for support, although, like me, they needed it desperately. Some of us are drowning in a sea of responsibility, but refusing to reach for a life raft—or even to admit that we need one—as the waters continue to rise above our heads. And though I didn't know exactly how at the time, I knew that I had to share my own revelation about support with other women around the world, because the solo struggle just ain't cute. Nor is it necessary. I want more women to see support differently, and that's the primary reason I launched my podcast, *Support is Sexy*, where I've interviewed more than five hundred successful women entrepreneurs all around the world about their journeys and about the important role support plays in their success.

Which brings us here, to this book. I am on a mission to empower unapologetically ambitious women like you, who are leaders in your careers, businesses, and lives, to embrace the power of support and collaboration and to get over "I Got It!" Syndrome. I believe enrolling others in your vision and being open to support in the many ways it may show up and lift you up are among the first steps to becoming truly empowered to realize your dreams for your life, to become an even better leader, to take care of yourself, and to step into all the joy and fulfillment that await you. Your fulfillment is limited when you choose to live a life where you feel you have to do everything on your own.

But maybe you're a woman who's reading this introduction right now and thinking: "This isn't for me. I'm good. I handle my business and take care of my family, too, without any support from anybody." Well, in case you need some extrinsic motivation, understand that, as women, we have incredible influence on those around us, whether we realize that power or not. We do a great disservice to our families, our communities, our colleagues, ourselves, less fortunate women whom we want to help, and the girls who look up to us when we play it small rather than ask for support in living fully, reaching higher, being our best, and serving from a place of abundance.

And this isn't a book about getting support just to get the best job or launch the billion-dollar business or find the perfect partner—although, sure, if that's your thing, then great! This is a book about you feeling whole rather than stretched thin, about you operating with a full tank rather than running on fumes trying to give to everyone else and request nothing, ever, for yourself. Everyone deserves support in reaching her next level, wherever you are, whoever you are. As women, especially now, we need one another, and we are more powerful together than alone. Think about all the magic you could experience in your life and create in the world if you just opened yourself up to support. Think of how much better you'd feel if you just had help!

This book is your guide to learning how to ask for the help you need in powerful ways. I have a simple H.E.L.P. framework that I use to support you with remembering to get over "I Got It!" Each letter in the acronym H.E.L.P. stands for a reminder that you should call on whenever you feel that resistance to support:

H. = Having it all doesn't mean doing it all alone.

The most powerful, successful people in the world know this secret: do not try to do it all alone. You're not being a hero, you are only hurting yourself. No matter how "independent" you think you are, wise women know that having it all doesn't mean doing it all alone. Get support, because you deserve it.

E. = Ask empowering questions.

Questions like, "Why am I so stupid?" "Why haven't I figured this out already on my own?" "Why don't I just give up?" are not empowering. Change your approach: Ask, "What am I missing?" "What do I get to learn in this moment?" "How do I get support for this?" Then live that question with enthusiasm and excitement rather than dread and frustration. Be open to the Universe's answer—it may surprise you

L. = Let go of the "how."

Let go of expectations about how the support you may need is going to come to you, what it looks like, when it will arrive, or who will have the answer or resource you need. Release those expectations, and let support show up for you as it's supposed to. You do not control the "how."

P. = Believe in the possibilities.

You must believe in the possibility that abundant support is out there and that it will show up for you. Your thoughts have much more power than you may be aware. So, reject any limiting beliefs and adopt what former Harvard Medical School Assistant Professor of Psychiatry Dr. Srinivasan S. Pillay calls "possibility thinking."[3] And then, make room for support in your life.

Each section of this book falls under one of those four categories in the H.E.L.P. framework, and each chapter offers a way that you can begin to get over "I Got It!" and break free of your own resistance to support. Also in this book—in addition to research on why support and connection are integral to our health and our survival as human beings (it's more than a theory, y'all!)—I thought it was important to give you inspiration from the real-life stories of other diverse, successful, and ambitious women executives, entrepreneurs, leaders, moms, and more, who have shifted their perspectives on support and changed their lives. Plus, I want you to take action! So, at the end of each chapter, I offer practical exercises so you can feel empowered to take action today and experience some of those life-changing results for yourself.

So, it's time to retire that tired-ass Superwoman cape, sis. Time to toss aside that "self-made" myth. The most successful leaders, businesspeople, and achievers in the world say that having coaches, mentors, mastermind groups, and a community of people to support them is what helped propel them to success and fulfillment. The best don't do it alone. Why should you? Even Oprah has Gayle.

It is my hope that with this book, you not only realize that you deserve support in every area of your life, but that you also realize a new way to embrace it as your superpower, and use it to create the life you truly want. I believe a cultural mindset shift around support will allow us all to connect (and reconnect) with one another again and tap into our compassion for ourselves and for others in this world that we all share. And it will be women, of course, who lead the way. If the COVID-19 pandemic has taught us anything by way of its impact on us globally, it's that we are far more connected to one another as human beings than we think, and we need that sense of connection more than we ever knew.

Now, I am not a psychologist, nor am I an "expert," but as my friend author-activist Marlon Peterson says, I am an expert on my own experiences. So, in this book, I share my experiences, the good and the not-so-great, wrapped in love, and laid bare in complete vulnerability. I open up about a lot of things I've never shared publicly, and I invite you to open your mind to a new possibility as you read them.

Because, after all, you have important things to do in this world, whether you're just getting warmed up in your career, you're a seasoned vet, or you're in a season of reinvention. You have brilliant ideas, you are unapologetically ambitious, and you are ready to make your own dent in the Universe. But you can't do all of that alone. And you shouldn't. You deserve support. And once you hold space for support differently, you will have no trouble boldly asking for what you need to manifest your vision into a powerful reality and to feel healthy and happy along the journey, no matter how bumpy it gets.

Because, listen . . .

Support is not weak.

Support is not a sign of incompetence.

Support is not laziness.

Support is Sexy!

And the sooner you get over "I Got It!" Syndrome, the sooner you'll realize that having it all doesn't mean doing it all alone!

SECTION ONE

Having It All Doesn't Mean Doing It All Alone

"I can be soft and still be successful."

—Artist and REALTOR® Maggie Minor on
Support is Sexy podcast

1

Define What "Having It All" Means to You

Can women really have it all? There is a constant debate about this. Some say we should accept that having it all simply is not possible. Some say you can have it all, but you cannot have it all at the same time.

I say both ideas can be true. It depends on you—what you believe and how you define "all" for yourself. Think about it: When you block out all the noise and the ideas other than your own of who you should be, where you should be, or how you should be, what does *your all* mean to you?

And that's the thing. Too often we define our all based on the lives we see other people living—whether we witness that life in person or we're just indulging as a voyeur on social media. We get so caught up in their moves, experiences, growth, and seeming accomplishments that we neglect to keep that same energy when it comes to investing in our own. When you allow yourself to get wrapped up in comparisons, you don't get fired up, you fizzle out.

For one, who knows what the true reality of that person's life is, the life that you're sitting there coveting with your eyes glued to the screen? It may be a hot mess on the inside, although it looks like one hell of a good time from the outside. Or, it might be perfect. The point is, you don't know, and really, it's none of your business. Sometimes a pretty picture is simply a pretty picture. Resist the temptation to project your insecurities on it one way or the other and create a story around how amazing that person's life is. Don't presume that they have it all. And don't presume that you never will. You really have no idea what the Universe has in store for you. While you're coveting someone else's pot of gold, yours may be just on the other side of that hill, or just beyond that door that's closer than you think. Someone else's joy and pursuit of their all should never deprive you of your own.

To be clear, this is something I've struggled with, too—comparing my life to the lives I see my beautiful and fabulous friends living via social media. It's never that I'm jealous of them . . . Okay, maybe sometimes, just a little, because who doesn't occasionally want to party like a rock star, travel to exotic locales, or be praised and rewarded for the work they do? But I remind myself that all our journeys are different, look different, and unfold differently.

Even more damaging than a case of the jellies as I scroll through my timelines are those sinister "shoulds" that start piling up in my mind with each and every swipe. "I should be in a position to do the same by now." "My business should be that successful." "I should have been invited to speak at that event." "I should be on that list of the Top Blah Blah Blah under Blah-zie Blah." I should, I should, I should . . . Before I know it, I've should-ed all over myself.

If you can relate, here's a gut check: No, you shouldn't. Not if those things don't truly align with and support who you are and the person you're becoming. And if they do align, trust that those opportunities will show up for you at the divine right time in the divine right form, because what's for you is for you—and no one can take that away from you. So turn those jellies into juice, let them serve as fuel for your own passions. Your friends who are living their best lives and pursuing their "all" are examples of what's possible for you.

What you have to do is get clear on what "all" means and looks like for you. Is it being a boss chick with a bomb career and running the show from the corner office? Is it having an amazing partner who loves, adores, and respects you, and a brood of beautiful children who make you proud to be their mommy every single day? Is it becoming the greatest entrepreneur and creating a product that changes the world as we know it? Is it becoming a monk and leaving your life in the big city behind to go live in an ashram in India? Is it all of the above? (That would be quite a feat, but you know what? I believe in you, so you go, girl!)

The thing is: it's up to you. "All" is an individual choice. It's not about who or what you're "supposed" to be based on someone else's rules or what society says; it's about who you feel you are meant to be based on your own deep-rooted desires and your vision for the life you want to create, the dreams you want to fulfill, the experiences you want to have, and the impact you want to make in this world.

So, at this point, you might be saying, "Okay, okay, that all sounds great; but how do I know what my all is?"

I'm glad you asked! Let's do an exercise to help you get clear and define what your "all" is at this time. And I say "at this time" because your all will continue to evolve. What you wanted at twenty years old is not necessarily going to be what you want at thirty, forty, sixty, eighty, and so on. As we live longer, some of our dreams and desires will evolve. Don't beat yourself up because something that may have seemed like everything to you a few years ago is no longer a high priority on your list. Things change, priorities shift. Allow it to do so naturally and continue to take shape as you grow as a person.

So, to start, grab a pen and a piece of paper or your journal so you can write some things down. And you'll notice me say this often throughout the book, "grab a pen and a piece of paper"—not only because I'm a writer and I have adored the art of writing since I was about three years old according to my mom; but because I believe writing things down gives them more power. (As a bonus, you can also download this exercise as a worksheet for free at elaynefluker.com and write your answers there.)

TAKE ACTION:
DEFINE YOUR "ALL"

Below, you'll see several categories of common areas of your life that you may want to set goals within. If something that's important to you isn't listed here, just add it on at the end. But this is where we're going to start.

For each category, you'll see a place where you'll write your particular goal, and then what's called your big-leap goal. Your big-leap goal is the goal that takes you a little bit further than your comfort zone when you think about it. Most of us, when asked about our goals, play it safe. Sure, you might think you're pushing yourself, but chances are you're not—not as far as you could. And that's normal. We all want to feel safe—part of it is human nature, part of it is ego. We want to know that we're not in danger of being eaten by a saber-toothed tiger, and we want to avoid being embarrassed or looking like a crazy person to those around us. But here, you're going to have the courage to really take that big leap in your mind. It's the only way you'll grow. So, write down something that makes you feel like it's damn near impossible for you to achieve that goal. In other words, does the goal make you squirm in your chair when the thought of it even enters your mind? That's it! Write that down!

After that, you're going to write down why this goal is important to you. The "what," which is the goal itself, is important, but the "why," the reason you want this, is paramount. Why do you want to achieve this goal? Why does it matter to you? Why will it matter in the world? Why will it make a difference?

Before we answer these questions, there are a few important things I want you to keep in mind.

1. **Be specific.** Specificity turns your dream into an objective, from a wish to a must. For example, if you say you want to be rich, I would ask you to be much more specific. How much money do you want to make: $10,000, $100,000, $1 million? And by when do you want to make this money? What's the date? This year? Within ten years? Be. Specific. Some might say this will lead you to be too rigid. On the contrary, I believe it will hold you accountable to your vision.

2. **Don't worry about the "how."** As I mentioned, the "what" and your "why" are incredibly important. But the "how"? Do not waste one second worrying about the "how" right now when it comes to your goals, and especially let it go when it comes to that big-leap goal that pushes you outside of your comfort zone. You will sabotage your thoughts by worrying about how you're going to make something become a reality that right now feels improbable, and it will cause you to hold back from daring to even dream of the possibilities. Truth is, you probably don't know

how; otherwise, you likely would have done it already, right? Trying to figure out the how before you have the insight and experiences that will inform the how is a poor use of your energy and doesn't support you. More likely, it is going to paralyze you and cause you to believe you have to wait until you have the entire path planned out before you even take that first step. Instead, focus on the goal and why it's important to you. The how will reveal itself as you bravely go along the journey.

3. **Set your intention.** When thinking about your why, think about your intention. What do you want to experience when it comes to this dream or goal? Or what do you want others to experience? I am very conscious of my intentions, whether I am trying something like establishing a new routine, going after a new goal in my business, or thinking about what type of experiences I want to create in my personal relationships. Your intention helps serve as a guidepost for you and helps remind you of your why, especially when challenges arise and attempt to take you off track. And trust me, challenges will arise.

Okay, ready? Grab that sheet of paper or your journal, and let's get started.

A. Your personal finance goal

1. What's the ideal number you want to achieve?
    Is there a certain amount you want to have in savings?
    A certain amount you want to invest? By when?

2. What's your big-leap goal? (Really want to push yourself on this one? Add a zero to that number above. Did that make you squirm? Good!)

3. Why? (Why this amount? Why is this important to you? Why does it matter? What will it allow you to do that you're not doing now?)

B. Your career or business goal

1. When you take away all the "shoulds," what is your vision for your career and the work you do? Or what is your dream business? (Again, be specific. Is it a certain position with a certain company? A certain salary or revenue for your business? A certain number of customers?)

2. What's your big-leap goal?

3. Why?

C. Your health goal

1. What does it look like? How do you want to feel when you reach this goal? (And be honest here—these goals are yours and yours alone. So, is your goal to look good naked? Write that down, girl! And then add a date.)

2. What's your big-leap goal?

3. Why is this important to you? (Again, no judgment here. And I say that because a lot of times it's not outside judgment that is the most challenging for us to overcome; it's our own self-judgment and criticisms.)

D. Your relationship goal

1. What is your vision for the relationships in your life? What does a loving relationship look like and feel like for you? (Is it a long-lasting romantic relationship? Is it having fun dating? It is bettering the relationship you're already in? You can also use this area to write about familial relationships or relationships with friends. How do those relationships support you? What are the ways they might need to heal?)

2. What's your big-leap goal?

3. Why does this matter to you?

E. Your personal development goal (courses, education, workshops, therapy, other wellness practices)

1. What are the ways that you want to grow as a person? What would you love to learn?

2. What's your big-leap goal?

3. Why are these important to you? Why will they help you grow?

F. Your impact goal

1. What impact do you want to have on the world? Who do you want to be? What do you want to be known for? How do you hope to contribute? Twenty years from now, what will people say about you?

2. What's your big-leap goal?

3. Why does this matter to you, and why will it matter to the world?

Again, if there's a category that you don't see here, write it down with the same format: the goal, by when, your big-leap goal, and your why for that goal.

Now, take some time to look back over what you just wrote. How do you feel? What was important to you? Any surprises? Any similar themes that run through the things you want to accomplish? Are your goals a reflection of your values, or are you dreaming based on someone else's standards? Make sure to be honest with yourself about this. Now is a good time to check in and get clear.

If you notice that a particular area is light on details, and you feel like you need to write on the back of the page for other areas, that's okay! That could just mean that the areas with less details aren't a high priority right now. Remember, priorities shift.

Also note that the dates for your "by when" questions are likely going to evolve. Don't stress out thinking you should accomplish everything on your list within the next year. Some may be ten months, others may be ten years. Again, this is okay.

After you've looked over what you've just written and given it some thought, walk away. That's right, put your list away and give yourself at least twenty-four hours to reflect on it lovingly, rather than with anxiety. Smile as you think about the dreams you now have written out, smile about the reason these dreams made your list. The idea of them should light you up.

Then, come back to the list and look again. Allow yourself to fill in more detail, to dream even bigger, leap—in your mind—even further. But resist the temptation to eliminate anything because it doesn't feel realistic or logical or because you don't know how you'd accomplish it. Don't forget: you're letting go of "the how." If you listed it there, it's there for a reason. That desire is in you somewhere. Let it ride for a while and see what develops and manifests in your life as time goes on. I find when I write things down and have it as part of my consciousness—even if I don't think it's a high priority at the time—I usually end up coming across a person, an opportunity, or some information eventually that aligns with that goal or desire, and it opens up new possibilities I hadn't considered before.

This exercise—which I often do as the first order of business when I lead vision board workshops and courses around the world from Spain to Morocco to South Africa to a small town in New Jersey—is inspired by my experience with Momentum Education, the transformational workshop that helped me shift my mindset around support and boldly declare my goals. I designed it to help you define what matters to you in your life right now and lead you to determine what "having it all" looks like for you. "Having it all" does not mean having every single thing in the world. It's about what is important to you.

And keep in mind, this list is not meant to capture every single moment of your future life. But it should help set the tone for you, put you in a space where your vision for your life, the person you want to become, and the things you want to experience begin to take shape.

The best part is, you don't have to try to achieve all this on your own. Support is out there and ready to show up for you, if you're open to it and you agree to get over "I Got It!" Syndrome.

2

Get Over "I Got It!" Syndrome

I hope the goal-setting exercise in the last chapter was super helpful for you. If so, I am thrilled!

If you're a woman who is already clear on your goals, that's great. You know who you are, you know what you want to accomplish, you know how far you want to go, and how fast you want to get there. But let me ask you: Are you traveling alone?

There is a saying often attributed to an African proverb that says, "If you want to go fast, go alone. If you want to go far, go together." For unapologetically ambitious women, sometimes we just know we gotta go! But too many of us are going too fast and pushing ourselves way too far without the support that is abundantly available for us. Instead of being open to it whenever it shows up for us in its many forms, our knee-jerk response to the offer of support is often, "I got it!" We some-times push the support away without even considering the possibility of how it may help us move forward, how it may relieve stress in our lives, or what a gift—whether big or small—it may be from the Universe in this very moment.

I call this knee-jerk rebuttal of support, "I Got It!" Syndrome. And it's something I struggled with my whole life until I knew better. And when you know better, you do better, right? But before I knew better, no matter how support showed up for me, I was quick to resist. Some-times it was the young guy who works at the grocery store, who offered to carry out my bags for me when he saw me hunched over, sweating and struggling to lug them all by myself. (Note, I'm not talking about some creepy stranger in the parking lot who is just looking for a way to get your attention or interact with you. This is the guy who works there!) Or those times when it was a colleague at the office who gener-ously said, "Let me know if you need any help with that project," when I was working late into the evening yet again. Other times it was a close girlfriend who could sense something was wrong with me and simply asked, "You okay, sis?" Before the offer could completely leave their lips, I pulled the trigger: "It's okay, I got it!"

And you know what? When I said "I got it," they believed me, and they left me to my own devices to figure out whatever it was on my own, whether they witnessed me struggle through it or not.

I've found that "I Got It!" Syndrome usually manifests in three dif-ferent ways for most of us:

1. **Defiant:** You respond with a strong "I got it!" when you want to make it clear to the other person that you are not stupid, needy, or weak, and that you're strong enough to do this on your own. You're the chief so-and-so, you're the director of such-and-such, you're the lead whatever in the

company—like, how dare they think you don't have it! This ego-driven response may also stem from the idea that no one else can do it as well as you can. You wouldn't dare let anyone else get it because you don't trust them to handle it.

2. **Defensive:** Whether you believe you have it or you don't, you're saying "I got it!" because you feel like you have something to prove—to yourself or to others in your life—and you're worried about how the other person may judge you for accepting support. "I got it!" is your tool for defending yourself against that judgment. It is your way of saying, "Back off!" This is especially true, I have found, for professional women in corporate spaces, where the fear is very real that accepting help will be interpreted as a sign of incompetence.

3. **Defeated:** You're so tired that you can barely muster the words, "I got it," but you do it because you feel like no one else will get it if you don't. Whether it's a big project at work that's going to keep you there all hours of the night or something as simple as answering the doorbell while everyone else in the house sits still, glued to the television or scrolling on their phones. You've become the go-to person who always gets it whether you want to or not, and at this point you've accepted your fate.

My "I Got It!" Syndrome has manifested in all three ways at different stages of my life. But here's the thing I later realized after becoming enlightened about my own adverse reaction to support and how that resistance was affecting me: most of the time, when I was sticking my chest out and exclaiming, "I got it!" I didn't really have it. I needed the support, but I didn't know how to accept it, so I simply refused it. You might be thinking: "Why didn't you just say 'yes'?" I couldn't. I didn't know how. As a matter of fact, it didn't even occur to me. Like most women, I wasn't conscious that this was a blind spot for me. I had tethered all these false meanings to support and what I believed it said about me. I'd rather have every muscle in my arms feeling like they're about to burst into flames from straining instead of saying, "Yes, thank you," to the gentleman working at the grocery store. I'd rather struggle through that project—likely taking twice as much time to complete it—than ask colleagues what their thoughts are on it. I'd rather uphold my image as the "strong one" in our sister circle and cry myself to sleep every night than tell my girlfriend that I need her support more than ever, but I'm just too damn embarrassed to ask her or inconvenience her.

"I Got It!" Syndrome causes you to miss out on opportunities to experience connection because you're worried about how it will make you look—either to the person offering support or the people you think are watching (even though, honestly, most people are paying you no mind). And though you might be inclined to say you struggle with "I Got It!" Syndrome because you're such an "independent woman," that resistance is really driven by ego and the questions that terrify most of us: "How will it look if I accept this offer of support? And what will that say about me?"

For starters, no matter how independent you think you are, or how many times you rock out to Destiny Child's classic "Independent Women" anthem from 2000 (shout out to DC!), independence is not real. We all depend on one another as human beings on this planet, including people we don't know and likely will never meet. Not convinced? Consider this: Do you make your own clothes? Do you grow your own food? Did you build the home you currently live in? Did you manufacture the machine that was used to make this book that you're reading? Nah, probably not.

Your claim of independence is your (in)security blanket, a work-around so that you don't have to learn how to accept support. And you wrap that blanket around you and wear it as your cape as you drive hard and push your way to success. I get it, sis, I've been there.

But as artist and REALTOR® Maggie Minor said so eloquently when I interviewed her for an episode of my *Support is Sexy* podcast, "I can be soft and still be successful."[1] Her words resonated deeply with me. Yes, I thought. It is a choice to be soft and successful. And I don't have to make it an either-or choice. I choose to make it a both-and choice.

So, even if you're a boss in whatever way you want to be (and maybe sometimes feel like you need to be), open yourself up to support by tapping into your feminine energy, which we'll explore more in the following chapter. The energy that is more receptive and open. Not only will it create space for people to show up for you, it may also transform your physical and mental health.

Giving into "I Got It!" Syndrome and not opening yourself up to support for whatever reason can lead you to feelings of isolation. At first, you rebuff the support, and then you're bothered because you're alone and you feel like you have no support. As a result of this isolation and the feeling that you're always doing it all alone, your stress level is likely to increase. And unhealthy stress kills. "We know that chronic stress can take a toll on a person's health," says Katherine C. Nordal, PhD, American Psychological Association's executive director for professional practice. "It can make existing health problems worse, and even cause disease, either because of changes in the body or bad habits people develop to cope with stress. The bottom line is that stress can lead to real physical and emotional health consequences."[2]

And with increased levels of unhealthy stress, you run the risk of slipping into depression, which the National Institute of Mental Health describes as "a mood disorder that may cause severe symptoms that can affect how you feel, think, and handle daily activities such as sleeping, eating, or working."[3]

Occasional feelings of sadness or mood swings are normal. But if you have been feeling this way consistently for more than two weeks—even if, on the outside, you're still "crushing it" at work—you could be experiencing depression.

First, there is no shame in this. I have been there as have more than 264 million people of all ages around the world, so you are not alone.[4] And, according to NIH, depression is more common among women than men,[5] likely due to certain biological, hormonal, and social factors that are unique to us as women, including, for example, those related to our periods, pregnancy, menopause, or issues of inequalities in the workplace. So, again, you are not alone, and depression doesn't say anything about who you are as a person or how strong or weak you are.

I have danced with depression for as long as I can remember; but as a child and well into my twenties and thirties, I didn't know (or didn't accept) what it was. Instead, I accepted what other people told me about my moods: that I was "too sensitive" or that, because I was "quiet" and rarely complained, I must be okay. Today, I realize that those moods, which I can only describe as emotional dips in an otherwise normal day, were likely part of my depression. The dips were my normal. And when I was fifteen years old, those dips—and the lack of support and understanding about what I was going through—led me to try to take my own life. I downed a handful of pills in an attempt to commit suicide because part of me wanted to disappear, while another part of me craved attention. I felt unseen in a home that was occasionally chaotic and not a space that prioritized affection, and I felt unloved and "unpretty" in a world that—especially at that time during the 1980s—didn't celebrate girls who looked like me with my dark skin, short, nappy hair, and full features.

I don't remember many details from that night. It's all a haze: my parents rushing me to the hospital, being given a slimy substance to make me vomit up the pills, and, however many days later, speaking to a psychiatrist, who pressed upon me the gravity of the situation—perhaps because it was apparent that I was completely numb to it all. "You do realize that you could have died, right?"

I am grateful that I survived that chapter of my life, in spite of the fact that, ironically, I didn't get any additional support regarding my suicide attempt after that night. I never saw that psychiatrist or any other after that first time because, as my mother would tell me many years later, they didn't think I needed one because I wasn't "crazy." And they were right: I was not crazy, but I was for sure depressed.

Only recently, just in the last six months of me writing this book, actually, did I really begin to accept that depression and anxiety are not conditions that are passing for me; they are—for whatever reason—a part of me, although they do not have control over me. Until that realization, I always thought I could just "get over it." Because, you know, I got it!

I am thankful my business and life coach, Margo Geller, knew that I didn't have it, and she revealed all the ways I had been struggling throughout my life to manage this on my own, and how it was, in fact, holding me down.

See, I believed I was doing all the "right things." I eat a plant-based diet, I meditate and have a spiritual practice, I exercise or move every single day, I work out with a trainer, I don't smoke and rarely, if ever, drink, I have a great social life and loving family, and I have been successful in advancing my career and growing my business. Girl, I was doing all the things! Yet I still struggled. As Margo helped me see, I had basically been successful climbing a mountain with twenty-five-pound weights on each leg. Weights I had been ignoring. She says it was remarkable that I had gotten as far as I had, "but imagine how far you can go if you let those weights go." Boom! That woke me up.

The way to remove those weights, for me at the time, was through trying prescribed medication that provided a boost in my serotonin levels. That seemed to help stabilize my moods. It didn't make me numb to my feelings and I wasn't skipping around like a carefree schoolgirl, which is what I worried about most. But I did notice that dips in my mood were much less frequent, especially during the extreme highs and lows that are part of entrepreneurship.

Some people are supported best by taking medication daily; others take it as needed. I take it as prescribed when needed. There is no shame in either option—it's about what works for you. I want to acknowledge that, because of the challenges with our health care system (at least in the United States), unfortunately, not all of us have the same access to doctors and medication. But do not let that stop you from getting the help you need to be your best, happiest, and healthiest self. Explore your options for support, some of which may be low or no cost.

Whatever your circumstances, if you think you may be experiencing depression, please seek help immediately from a physician, a therapist, or other trusted resources, who can support you and guide you through this period. Do not try to do this on your own. There is help available for you, and at the end of this chapter, you can find phone numbers and websites for hotlines that you can reach out to immediately.

Depression and its symptoms are real. This is not the time for "I Got It!" Syndrome. And now that you've read this, you know how urgent it is that you get support. You might choose to ignore it, but you can't un-know it. This is especially important for us to recognize as women today. We are stressed more than ever and doing more than ever. That doesn't come without a cost. And, sadly for some of us, it's costing us our lives.

This is a serious matter, sis. So when it comes to support during this time, instead of "I got it," please, lean in to "I receive it."

TAKE ACTION:
LET GO OF "I GOT IT!"

One of the best ways to get over "I Got It!" Syndrome is to push yourself to think of ways that you can get support for the things you want to (or need to) accomplish in your life. This may be challenging, but again: push!

Let's take a look at the goals you wrote down at the end of Chapter 1. Under each goal, write down at least three ways that you can get support for that goal. Think broadly. Don't limit yourself to the people you already know or the knowledge you already have. For example, if there's someone specific or in a certain field that you think you'd benefit from meeting or getting to know (yet you have no idea how you'd meet this person), write it down. If there's some education you have to acquire but you may have no idea how you're going to afford the course because of your current circumstances, write it down. You've let go of the "how." Write it down, then take the first step you know to take. The path becomes clearer with each step, and your confidence will grow with each step. Best part? Because you're now open to support, the right support will show up for you in ways you never expected.

RESOURCES FOR SUPPORT

National Suicide Prevention Hotline 1-877-275-TALK (8255)
    (available twenty-four hours a day, seven days a week),
    https://suicidepreventionlifeline.org/.
The Veterans Suicide Hotline (Veterans Crisis Line): 1-800-273-8255
    (available twenty-four hours a day, seven days a week),
    http://www.veteranscrisisline.net/.

Lesbian, Gay, Bisexual, Transgender, Queer, and Questioning
(LGBTQ) Suicide Hotline (the TrevorLifeline): 1-866-488-7386
(available twenty-four hours a day, seven days a week),
https://www.thetrevorproject.org/get-help-now/.

For support outside of the United States, contact Befrienders
Worldwide, an international suicide prevention organization at
befrienders.org.

Betterhelp, an online platform that offers access to licensed, trained, and
accredited psychologists, therapists, social workers, and counselors,
according to the company's website, https://www.betterhelp.com.

3

Tap Into Your Feminine Energy

Look, I understand: "I got it" lets people know you're a woman who knows how to handle her business and make it happen, right? Most times, you wear it as a badge of honor, especially if you're a woman who is in a leadership role. If they see you getting too much support, it will make you look weak or incompetent. So, instead, you show up as the strong, powerful, always-pulled-together chick who needs no one. And when you do run into a roadblock, you'll just struggle through it and figure it out on your own, no matter how long it takes or how taxing it is, in order to maintain control and keep up appearances.

Sure, this is one way of doing it—a very masculine way. Not male, masculine. Each of us has masculine energy and feminine energy within us, with the masculine energy usually showing up as the driver, go-getter, in-control problem-solver, and the feminine energy typically more nurturing, empathetic, intuitive, open, and receptive. Depending on the circumstance, moment, or relationship, one energy may show up more often in your life than the other. As unapologetically ambitious women, though, many of us rely on our masculine energy to get ahead, and completely ignore our feminine. Ask yourself: How am I choosing to show up?

Before I learned how to be comfortable with support and receiving it, my masculine energy—especially as it related to my career and later to my business—was often on 110 percent. The story I told myself was that this is who I had to be in order to be successful. I wasn't mean, but I definitely tapped into the masculine energy. I had my head down, guard up, and my armor strapped on tight. I presented as strong, always. And I was determined to prove I was "independent."

Did it work? In some ways, yes, especially as it relates to my career. I rose quickly through the ranks as a magazine and digital editor and writer—from intern to executive editor—and I was a prolific producer and content creator at major media outlets until I decided to become a full-time entrepreneur. But being led by my masculine energy is not the only way and, for me, no longer the ideal way. Plus, it was exhausting. I don't want to deny my feminine energy in any part of my life just because I'm fearful that it will make me look weak. In the same way that I love my strength, my drive, and my ambition, I want to be comfortable embracing my vulnerability, my humanity, my softness, and to be open to support—knowing that I can still thrive. I now love that part of myself.

I was first called out on leading with my masculine energy when I was part of a twelve-month mastermind group in 2016 with about ten other women entrepreneurs. As part of our time together, the leader of our mastermind group brought in other powerful women, who had expertise in different areas and who could support the members of the group with our varying businesses. That year, on a cold winter's day in a New York City office building conference room, one of the women who walked in to share her expertise was Danielle Mercurio. Danielle is a confidence coach and meditation guide who empowers individuals to be successful, intentional, and to live life on purpose. She is also an astrologist, and on this day, she was there to give us a read.

Armed with just our birthdays, time and place of birth, and maybe a little bit about the work we did, Danielle told each woman in the group what she picked up on about them and what may be a blind spot blocking us from growing our businesses or creating the life we really wanted. When she came around to me, I immediately felt my body stiffen in the conference room swivel chair where I was perched near the end of a long table. Although I was trying my best to look relaxed, the armor was definitely on that day. Danielle saw right through me, and she shared, in short, that she felt I was leading with my masculine energy. I needed to learn how to tap into my feminine energy if I really wanted to succeed, she told me; otherwise, I would always have a block there. After hearing her feedback, of course, I was—offended!

I didn't understand what it all meant. My first reaction was to think she meant I was presenting as masculine, or male, which is not how I see myself. But as Danielle continued to explain, it made more sense. I had been leading with my masculine energy without realizing it, and it was actually part of the reason I had always been resistant to support—and, as a result, was stressed and exhausted. I was trying desperately to force my business to be successful rather than being open to discovering and receiving signs of the *ways* it could be successful. New ideas—and support—would never be able to get in if I stayed rigid, guarded, and closed off to it.

That conversation has stuck with me ever since I first met Danielle in that chilly conference room in 2016. Since then, I believe I've been more conscious of allowing my feminine energy to take the lead, or at least reveal that part of myself more consciously. I've done tons of research on my own to learn more about this, what it all means, and how I can be better at it, but I haven't quite nailed it. (Just the fact that I used the phrase *nailed it* right here probably indicates that I still have a lot of work to do, and I welcome it.)

So, when, three years after our initial interaction, I asked Danielle to be a part of this book and take a deeper dive on what she believes masculine and feminine energy mean and how they impact us as unapologetically ambitious women, I could barely wait for her to get comfortable in her chair for our Zoom call before I got started.

"All right, so the first question I want to ask you is how do you define feminine energy?" I ask.

"I believe feminine energy will always be evolving, and I think as you step into it, you'll start to understand it more and more," Danielle says calmly with a knowing smile. "It's that part of us that's kind of how we are behind closed doors. It's not always the person that we lead with when we're out and about during the day. It's when we have that quiet time, when we have that stillness, and we have that moment to listen to that inner voice inside of us that feels like guidance or feels like *us*. Right?"

I nodded.

"When you say, who are you, when we feel out that space—if we can get there—that's our feminine. It's kind of this state of flow that we can access," she continues. "It's also very similar to the notion of fertility in a way. We technically need masculine to create something, but feminine is being patient and [giving] it time to evolve and develop. So this notion of femininity is very related to fertility, because femininity is about growth and evolution and understanding that it's going to take time."

Danielle says, if feminine is nighttime and bringing what she calls "moon energy," then masculine brings "sun energy."

Masculine energy "is who we are during the day," she explains. "It's the actions that we take. It's where we get our drive, where we get our ambition. It's what fuels things and allows things to move forward."

Danielle's point is an important distinction to understand. This conversation about masculine and feminine energy, as I learned after our first encounter in that conference room, is not a conversation about gender. "I think we're starting to recognize in general that gender can mean so many things," she says. "We're not defined by what our human vessel looks like per se. And it's the same thing with feminine and masculine energy. It has nothing to do with gender and everything to do with essence and energy. But for some reason, our patriarchal society kind of labeled what the energies would be through our human form through gender, which has skewed us."

If this is all getting a little too woo-woo for you, let me break it down: feminine energy is not about getting your nails done, and masculine energy is not about chopping wood. That's not it at all. "It's about tapping into the intuitive, subtle, soft energy for the feminine," Danielle explains to me. "And when the masculine comes in, it's about that energy of doing. We need both to be harmonious."

"When we are so tapped into our masculine, we are in a mindset of 'I have to do it myself. I have to create, I have to generate,'" says Danielle. "When we're tapped into our feminine, we become, 'I'm in this mode of receiving. I receive support, I receive inspiration, I receive guidance.' When we allow that, we can kind of lean back, and we can see what it feels like to ask and let it happen."

To help you tap into your feminine energy with ease (because, chances are, you already have the masculine mastered), Danielle suggests you find opportunities to either be still (like meditation, reading a book, or taking a relaxing bath) or find a way to be peacefully creative (like gardening, cooking, or making a piece of art). Anything where you can, as she says, "take away that masculine element."

Find a way to be present and nurture yourself in whatever form works for you. So, if the thought of sitting in a corner and meditating gives you more anxiety than a sense of peace, find *your* peace.

When I first met Danielle in New York, I definitely wasn't at peace. I was struggling hard with my current business and didn't even know if I wanted to continue. Ironically, I had this other idea in my mind that I just couldn't shake. It was a concept called *Support is Sexy*, but I didn't yet know if that could be a "real business," so I focused on the one I was building at the time—an online video network for women of color called ChicRebellion.TV.

When I ask Danielle how she was able to detect this struggle within me three years earlier, she explains I had this "I have to do it myself" vibe.

"I could feel this kind of essence of, 'What do I need to do? Tell me what's next and I'll do it.' And that's great," she says, "but there also was this guard up that made me believe that even if I gave you all of those things—or if anyone gave you those things—you still wouldn't fully integrate them because there was a missing layer of you understanding how to tap into that notion of support and trust."

Her analysis was spot on and, honestly, sometimes it is still my default. The difference is, armed with this new information, I now know how to pause, shift, be open, and receive.

I believe that moment with Danielle back in 2016, when she challenged me to be more aware of my energy, is the reason I was open enough to even mention the *Support is Sexy* concept during one of our later mastermind meetings. I wasn't pitching it; I was actually showing it in practice. From what I recall, one of the women in the group mentioned how overwhelmed she felt when it came to having the time she felt she needed to build and grow her new business and take care of things at home with her family. I mentioned my *Support is Sexy* concept, a phrase I had been using as a mantra to remind myself to ask for support, and I saw the face of every woman in that room light up.

And here we are.

TAKE ACTION:
PUT YOURSELF FIRST

While building a new habit of being open to your feminine energy will take time and, quite honestly, practice, there are some actions you can take as a first step to get you started along that path. And that first step is to put yourself first, especially first thing in the morning.

Think about it: What's the first message you're giving to yourself when you wake each morning? Is it one of self-love and reflection, one that isn't tainted by the outside noise, chaos, and influences of morning television or your morning scroll through the 'gram? Or are you sitting on the toilet and taking in the lives of other people before you even start your day? No judgment. We just want to do a check-in, right?

Instead of grabbing your phone as soon as you rise, lie in bed for just thirty seconds and say one reason you are grateful for that day. Just one to start your day from that place and with that energy. A ritual that I have practiced for years is that, before my feet hit the floor, I simply whisper, "Thank you." I know whoever needs to hear it will.

Another powerful way to start your day is to do as Danielle does every morning: she takes a moment to look at herself in the mirror and actually see herself. Not seeing or focusing on anything that she may perceive as imperfections or flaws, just taking in her beautifully human self. Have you paused long enough to look yourself in the eye lately? Have you seen and admired your beautifully human self, without mention or even thoughts of all the things you perceive as flaws or imperfections or things you want to change? Have you ever looked at *you* and said, "You are glorious!" and wholeheartedly meant it? Why not start today?

If this feels a little too overwhelming—and I understand if it does, because loving up on ourselves doesn't always come easily when we're out of practice—then start simple. Each morning, as you brush your teeth, use that time to look at yourself in the mirror and repeat: "I love you. You are beautiful. You are worthy. You are such a great person. You are doing your best. You deserve support. And you're going to have an awesome day!" over and over for as long as you're brushing those pearly whites. Doing this while you brush your teeth makes it a habit because, I'm presuming here, you're going to brush your teeth every morning. So, why not let it be a trigger for your affirmations? Also, you're probably going to sound ridiculous brushing and saying affirmations—and that's a good thing! It doesn't mean you're not taking the practice seriously, but it adds some levity to it that may make you feel more comfortable, and even make you smile. And what a beautiful way to start your day. I do this practice while flossing—so you can imagine how ridiculous I sound. But, hey, it helps me connect with the feminine in me—that loving, connected part of me—and it makes me giggle. That's what counts.

4

Retire Your Cape

As women, we are making more professional strides than ever—graduating with college degrees at higher rates than men, rising in corporate spaces, launching businesses, and becoming entrepreneurs at rates five times the national average in the United States, making history in political offices around the world, and making an impact on a global scale in a variety of fields. We are also juggling many of the responsibilities that typically still fall heavily on the shoulders of women in our society. We manage the household, take care of our families, have and raise children, and care for our aging parents while also trying to take care of ourselves. (Notice I put "take care of ourselves" last on the list here, not because it should be last, but because, unfortunately for many of us, it often is.)

Add to this our own struggles with comparing our lives, our accomplishments, and our abilities to juggle it all with our "friends"—whether in real life or on their social media highlight reels—and the stress of trying to keep everything together (and make it all look pretty and effortless). It's enough to drive anyone crazy.

We spend so much of our time trying to be Superwoman that many of us are dangerously flying at breakneck speeds straight toward a brick wall without even realizing it. We just know that there's a lot to do, and we feel like the only person who can get it done.

Here's the trouble with Superwoman: she's not real.

Literally, she is not real. She is a fictional character from DC Comics that first appeared in the 1940s. Yet many of us aspire to be Superwoman in all areas of our lives today—work, family, church, at our kids' school, with our friends, you name it. We tie on the cape and try to be everything to everybody everywhere. And the message we get, and have been getting for decades since at least the era of second-wave feminism in the 1960s, is that this is what we're supposed to do as women. All of it!

The Superwoman complex—also known as the Superwoman syndrome, where you feel like you can and should do everything on your own—will do you in.

"Superwoman complex" was a term first popularized in the 1970s as more women transitioned from solely filling the role of devoted housewife to the additional role of career woman. But this didn't mean that many women were letting go of what they saw as their responsibilities as wives and moms and homemakers. They added to those responsibilities with the demands of a career. And that sense of obligation still has a hold on many of us today—times ten!

Psychologist Dr. Zoe Shaw, host of the podcast *Dr. Zoe Show: Redefining Your Superwoman,* speaks often about the Superwoman complex on her podcast and in her work with clients.[1]

Admitting to being a "recovering Superwoman" herself, Dr. Zoe says most of us give into this complex because of unspoken pressures that we succumb to in our society. I chatted with her while she was home in California about the reasons we feel obligated to walk around with an "S" on our chest. She first cited the cultural double standard that exists for men and women—the one that positions men to be celebrated and women to be shamed for doing the exact same thing.

For example, she says, when one of her male friends, who is a radio station owner, a DJ, and a single dad, takes his young daughter to work or to gigs with him, everyone celebrates him for what a great dad he is. "I said to [my friend], 'You know, it's funny because when you bring your daughter to work, everybody thinks that's so adorable. All the women want to help you and hang out with your daughter.'"

But Dr. Zoe also pointed out to her friend that if she—a married, loving mom of five children, ages six to twenty-five, and a busy career woman—were to do the same and take her youngest child to the office, the outcome would likely be very different. "If I bring my kids to work, there's this tone of, 'That's not professional.'" People might never say they see a problem with it, that they perceive her differently, or that they're judging her; but the judgment would certainly be felt and likely cause her to think that she may have done something wrong. Most of us know exactly what that judgment feels like, whether we sense it from the people around us or it's a story we tell ourselves.

"The strongest held rules are never spoken," Dr. Zoe says of the double standard.

The second reason Dr. Zoe believes we succumb to the Superwoman complex is fear of what it means if we don't get it all done. What does it say about who we are as women, as mothers, as business or career women, as individuals who fight for our rights, and who have benefited from the work of other women who fought fiercely and tirelessly on our behalf for generations before us, to have options but to not take advantage of all of them?

"Any good thing has unintended consequences," Dr. Zoe says, using the feminist movement as an example. We are now overwhelmed by all the things we can do and feel like we should do. Ultimately, we don't feel like we have a choice but to do it all. As a result of the unreasonable pressure we put on ourselves, she says, women now have more instances of cardiovascular disease, increased stress, and higher anxiety. "We're grateful we have choices, but our job is to take care of ourselves."

Along with a sense of obligation that we may have to do it all, Dr. Zoe says it's also an innate part of us as women to want to support and nurture those around us. "We were made to be nurturers, and that is good and okay," she says. "I believe that we need to honor our inherent femininity as women instead of always trying to step outside of it. [Because] we are nurturers, we tend to be more emotionally aware of the people in our lives. And that is a burden. It takes up emotional space in our lives. So, by being concerned about certain things with our children, about our family members, whether it's caretaking just for our nuclear family or even extended family members, women tend to carry the burden for that."

To keep from getting swallowed up by Superwoman complex, Dr. Zoe says we have to first recognize that there's a problem and then commit to making adjustments, which is something she helps her clients do regularly.

"A perfect example is: I was talking to a woman, and she's a manager at her company," Dr. Zoe explains. "And as the manager, she has certain standards for people she manages that they should have to do in the company. She requires all of the people she manages to answer every single email they get every single day." Sounds reasonable enough. But

Dr. Zoe says the issue is, this manager is also holding herself to this same expectation—which isn't reasonable when all is taken into consideration. "What she said is, 'Well, I expect them to do it. And as their manager I should do it as well.' Now, she gets *four times* the emails that they get. So I started to talk to her about that.

"I asked her, 'So, how many emails do you get a day?' And she said something like two hundred, something ridiculous. And I said, 'Is it realistic for you to actually be able to answer every single one every single day and adequately get all the rest of your work done?' The simple answer was no. And yet you have that expectation for yourself that doesn't meet reality. In the middle of that is Superwoman syndrome. That's how I try to help people. Look at what you're doing, look at the balls that you're juggling. Is it realistic?"

I know what you're likely thinking, because I thought the same thing: What if you've been doing it this way for so long that you know it's going to feel impossible to change? Not just for yourself. You may also be wrapped up in what changing yourself will mean to everyone else in your life, personally and professionally.

"Well, everyone's resistant to change for different reasons, and we all create our own stories about why we can't or shouldn't or aren't, [and why] it's not okay for us to change," Dr. Zoe says when I ask her how we get over this excuse. "The first thing I always say is: you are never obligated to be the same person you were yesterday. That's your own obligation you're putting on yourself, number one. And then number two: if you aren't changing, then you're not growing."

In other words, it's time to retire that Superwoman cape, love. Take it off, fold it up, and drop it off at your local Goodwill. Or, better yet, burn it so another woman doesn't scoop it up. Instead, put an "S" on your chest for *support* and use your superpowers to courageously change in your life, starting today. It's time to soar in a different direction.

TAKE ACTION:
PRIORITIZE AND OPTIMIZE

I know that even if you have the best intentions of not overwhelming yourself by taking on anything and everything that you feel needs to be handled in all areas of your life, your to-do list probably has your obligations on lockdown. While I'd never suggest that an unapologetically ambitious woman like you totally discard your to-do lists (because I don't want those kind of problems), I do love what Dr. Zoe says we need to do with our lists in order to get over Superwoman syndrome. Prioritize. For real. Dr. Zoe says there are three steps to this process.

1. Make a list (of your activities) and check it twice. "Let's say a woman has a priority of having dinner every night as a family. Not working on the weekends. Meditation. Let's just say different priorities. Everyone's going to have different ones. Whatever is in her life that's really important to her," Dr. Zoe explains. "I would want her to sit down and list all the activities she does every week. Now, let's say we look at this list of activities, and this woman says that it's a priority for her to have dinner every night with her family, yet she's got something scheduled most evenings, and what she's really doing is running through the drive-through at McDonald's. And so then there's that sense of disconnect with her priorities, which she's probably not even aware of, but it's this nagging feeling she has. What she holds as a priority is not in alignment with her activities. And so when you draw a line from those priorities, and then you recognize that some of those things that you have listed as activities are not directly attached to your priorities, then it's time to start culling your activities. This can be hard."

2. Cull your activities. As you're looking at your activities and measuring them against what you say are your priorities, you want to be honest with yourself about whether they align or not. If they don't, only you have the power to make a change, prioritize your list, and optimize your time and energy by eliminating the activities that do not serve you or your priorities. This not only keeps you from falling victim to the Superwoman complex, it keeps you from beating yourself up when you inevitably fail to live up to what you've said are your priorities because your activities are sabotaging you. It also lets you channel your energy toward what really matters.

Dr. Zoe says, for example: "If you decide, you know what, soccer really is a big priority in my life. I want my kids to play soccer six nights a week. Well, then, is that a bigger priority than family dinners? And it's okay if you change your priorities, but you need to make sure that they're in line, because when they are in line, then you feel balanced; when they're not in line, you do not feel balanced."

She tells women: "You should be regularly writing down your activities and regularly questioning, 'Is this still in line with my priorities?'"

3. Ask for help. Dr. Zoe says after you cull your activities, it's time to ask for some help. "Once you've figured out maybe some things that you need to cull, then it might be time to call a family meeting, especially if you're going to be cutting out things that don't just pertain to yourself. Or maybe it's that you need to bring in some extra help. You need to ask your spouse for help for something, or you need to hire somebody, or you need to delegate some things to your family members."

One thing Dr. Zoe warns against, however—for yourself and for your family—is that you don't attempt sweeping changes all at once. Don't go crazy. In your excitement about this exercise, you might feel inspired to say something like everyone in your family has to go to bed an hour earlier because you want to wake up an hour earlier and go to the gym every morning and work out starting *tomorrow* so that your activities align with your priority of getting in shape. While that's an admirable goal, and it might seem reasonable when you're writing it on your list, is this a realistic adjustment for you and for your family to make overnight?

Instead, Dr. Zoe says, take small steps and celebrate the small wins along the way to keep yourself motivated. Sweeping changes are difficult to maintain. Start with a small first step. Instead of sending your family's system of operations into complete upheaval so you can head out to the gym and work out for an hour every morning, how about working out for fifteen minutes at home? It still counts, and it's a minor adjustment for your family.

"That woman who works out fifteen minutes a day or fifteen minutes every other day, what happens is she gets consistent with it," Dr. Zoe says. "She developed confidence in those fifteen minutes, because it's pretty easy. And all of a sudden, she has a deeper desire and motivation to work out and will probably naturally start adding more time. When you try to create those huge changes, it feels overwhelming, because there's a reason why you're doing the things you do right now. You have a system, and your system is always trying to have this equilibrium. When we change, our system naturally tries to bring us back for whatever reason. There are a lot of reasons why we do what we do. To really work against that, you have to make the changes very small so that the system is not hugely disrupted. Then you can grow over time and your whole family doesn't have to change their schedule for you to work out fifteen minutes a day."

Little by little, a little can become a lot.

5

Fall Back

Just in case there is any confusion, I am not suggesting that you blow off any of your responsibilities as a woman, a wife, a mom, a daughter, a sister, a friend, a lover, a leader, as a beautiful, whole human being who is making a contribution to the world, or as someone who is unapologetically ambitious. I understand. You're a busy woman who is filling multiple roles in your life, and there are going to be times when you may need to lean in. But, for the sake of your mental health and wellness, there are also times when you have to make the brave and conscious decision to fall all the way back.

Such was the case for first-time mom Kongit Farrell. "I told my husband, 'Look, I'm a strong Black woman, but I'm not *that* strong. I'm going to need your help,'" Kongit says, laughing. She is the founder of the Inspired Journey Counseling Center in Los Angeles and, when we spoke online for this book, new mom to a three-month-old. Kongit said her husband, who happens to be white, understood because she was forthright about what she needed, and he made sure she had that support.

As a licensed marriage and family therapist, Kongit knows the value of falling back, making room for support, and bravely asking for it. However, for many of her clients—who include highly ambitious and successful women who are trying to figure out why they can't "have it all and do it all"—she says there are a few common factors that block these women from falling back and accepting support, even when it's offered. Below are the ones she wants to make sure you're aware of.

1. **Mindset.** Kongit agrees with Dr. Zoe and says many ambitious women have a view that being a feminist or a "modern woman" means that you should be capable of doing everything on your own. As a result, you shun support and are sometimes even offended by the offer. "It's like, if you're not rolling up your sleeves, pumping your muscles, and you're not doing it all yourself, then somehow you're not living up to this feminist standard or ideal," she says.

   The cure, she suggests, is to reframe your thinking around what it means to be a woman today and to not be defined by how much you're accomplishing solo. Instead of harboring fear about what getting support says about you and that in some way it paints you as less of a woman, Kongit says women need to realize that, if you're stressed or sick or things aren't working in your life, you can (and must!) make a change. Sometimes that change involves support from others. In other words, you are not doomed to struggle and suffer alone just to prove what a badass feminist you are.

2. **Experience.** Let's face it. Every request for support unfortunately is not always met with a loving response. So Kongit says women who may have been "burned" in

the past or had a disappointing experience after asking for support are understandably apprehensive about asking for it again. "I think that women who tend to be ambitious are a certain kind of woman. Usually they're bright, they're industrious, they have a vision about things, and you know what that also attracts? Jealousy. A lot of these women have been in mastermind groups or groups where they've had these interesting ideas and someone has stolen them. Or they've reached out for support, and someone has hated on them. They've had this experience of being burned when asking for help. So, what they decide is, 'Well, then, I'm not going to ask for help again,' instead of saying, 'Okay, how can I be more mindful about who I lean out to?'"

It happens. But don't give up. Instead, be more thoughtful about the requests you make and to whom you make them. "Part of what makes leaning out successful is also the mindfulness and the conscious curating of your relationships," Kongit says. Consider: Are you surrounded by people who lift you up, who want to support you, who hold you to your highest, who aren't jealous or insecure about your success or even your dreams of success? Do you have mentors or advisors in your life (no matter what age you are) who can offer guidance and who want to see you win when it comes to your work and to your wellness? If not, it's time to take stock of your circle and adjust accordingly. Toxic relationships taint everything around them. Let go of the relationships that no longer serve you, and distance yourself from people who don't have the capacity to support your vision. Most important: Don't let them stop you from getting the support you need.

3. **FOMO.** Kongit says another factor that stops some ambitious women from leaning out is the fear of missing out, or FOMO, as it's often called. In this case, though, I guess it's more like FOLO, a fear of *leaning* out. However you acronymize it, the idea that you have to keep pushing, plowing through, suffering mentally and possibly physically in order to accomplish your goals and not miss out on the rewards is a dangerous narrative—one that will have you burning out, breaking down, and in Kongit's office for an emergency therapy session before you know it. It's also one that's driven by ego because there's a belief that you alone are responsible for your success. Yes, of course, you have ownership over what you do, how passionately you pursue your goals, and how committed you are to your work, but Kongit reminds ambitious women that no matter how hard you're pushing or striving, there are always other elements at play when it comes to your success—something Kongit says can be difficult for driven and successful women to accept.

What we each have to realize, she says, is that our lives have seasons. "Even some top female entrepreneurs [and women you admire for their public successes] have had seasons in their lives where they were working hard and being consistent, but things weren't manifesting," Kongit says. Each of us experiences our own winters, springs, summers, and falls. It's cyclical. Fall and winter—which are usually the toughest for us—are seasons of releasing, transition, reflection, and recharging. During this time, Kongit says we have to "do the work of winter."

"The work of the fall and the winter is reckoning work. Taking a pause. Falling back. Evaluating things. Saying:

'Okay, where am I now? What kind of seeds do I want to plant now? What do I want spring to look like, that next season?'" Instead of attempting futilely to avoid your seasons or trying to rush through them (and, as a result, stressing yourself out), embrace each season as a gift. "There are going to be seasons where you're pushing hard and great things are happening; there are going to be seasons where you're pushing hard and nothing's happening. The more that you can get in touch with that life rhythm, I think the easier the journey is going to be."

And Kongit says don't waste time coveting other people's "spring" or "summer," which tend to be the seasons when things are lighting up, blooming, or maybe even on fire, in a good way. Again, your season is for you, their season is for them. Instead, she says, "If you do the work of winter, you're going to have a long, abundant spring."

Whatever season you are currently experiencing at this point in your life, remember that falling back doesn't mean that you've fallen *off.* Your need to pause, hit the brakes, and ask for support doesn't indicate that you are a failure or that you're not worthy of your position, your accomplishments, or anything else. You are falling back for your own sake and sanity. Whether that's a weeklong solo getaway, a quiet evening alone, an hour where you turn your phone off and ignore all the bells, pings, whistles, and notifications, ten minutes of silence, or a one-minute guided meditation. Whatever it takes to support you in being your best, healthiest self holistically, be like Nike and just do it. Never mind what other people may think. When you give more value to what people think or say about you than you give to what's best for you, you are on a slippery slope, my sister.

Other people are not looking at you. Or, you know what? So what if they are? No matter who it is—family, friend, boss, or boo—this is about you, your health, your wellness, your sanity, your time here on this earth. And think about it: Would you rather people look at you and judge you while you're taking a break, falling back, being self-reflective, and getting the support that you need, or would you rather them look at you and judge you when you're lying in your coffin because the stress and anxiety got the best of you?

Make a conscious decision to fall back, and when you do, you'll learn to create space for support to abundantly flow in.

TAKE ACTION:
LET IT GO

As a successful, ambitious, badass woman, I know you wanna do it all. (You're a boss! Message received.) But I hope, as you've read up until this point, that you're starting to realize some of the ways your badassery could lead you to burnout. And I don't want that for you or your life. There's a better way. So I'm going to present you with what might be the toughest challenge of your life for this exercise: I'm going to challenge you to let some stuff go.

That's right, pull out that to-do list we've been chatting about in the last couple chapters and choose a to-do that you're going to let go—especially if it's one related to your business or career. Hold on to anything related to fun, relaxation, or connecting with family and friends, unless there's a sense of overwhelm attached to that one. (If you have any negative feelings attached to something that's supposed to be a good thing, maybe it's not so good for you right now.)

Either way, don't panic. You don't have to let this thing go forever (unless you decide it's a goner). Let's say you'll let it go for the next thirty days. You're going to put that thing on hold and completely push it to the side for the next thirty days so you can create some breathing room on your list and in your life.

Think of it this way. What's on the list that's a "nice to do" but not a must? What's an area where you kind of already felt like you've overextended yourself, but you're sucking it up and doing it anyway? What event have you agreed to attend (or maybe even keynote!) that you can responsibly tell them you've determined that, actually, no, you're not going to be able to make it this time?

It can be tough, I know. Ambition, FOMO, FOLO, obligations—they all stick to our to-do lists like glue. Don't worry. Those to-dos will be there. And if not, new ones are sure to appear. Trust me. Give yourself the gift of falling back and taking some time to reflect, assess what season you're in, and be open to what is set to bloom without you having to force it or "make it happen." You may discover that some of the things that you felt were matters of life and death if you didn't take them on aren't even that important to you, after all.

And as you're going through this exercise, remember, *you* get to decide what *really* matters to you, and you also get to bravely let the others go. No one else. You.

6

Stop Being "The Strong One"

When I think about the concept of a "boss," I think of my best friend, April McKoy Robinson. April grew up in Kingston, Jamaica, moved to the United States to be with her mom at age six, and lived in the Bronx, New York, until she went off to college and met me and the other members of our tightly knit sister circle at Hampton University in Hampton, Virginia.

Today, April has a master's degree in education, and she is the founder and principal emeritus of the Urban Assembly Gateway School for Technology in New York City—one of the most celebrated schools in the state and a leader in teaching high school students skills in STEM (science, technology, engineering, and mathematics) that they can use in the real world. (She created an actual school, y'all!) I still recall sitting with her in a beat-up little coffee shop in Fort Greene, Brooklyn, years earlier when the school was just a concept that she was pitching. And I giggle when I think about the many hilarious stories she used to tell me and my girlfriends, many, many years before, about how she was not at all, *ahem*, "focused" in high school.

But now, not only is April's dream school up, running, and experiencing much success, she has built something else magnificent during that same period: a family. She and her wonderful husband, Marc Andre Robinson, who is a celebrated artist, professor, and avid fisherman, live in Brooklyn with their two beautiful young sons. And April is now turning around a whole new school.

I am in awe of all teachers and educators, really, because I think the profession is one of the most crucial in our society. These professionals deserve far more acknowledgment and compensation than they currently receive. Teachers are literally shaping our future in what is often grueling, sometimes thankless, sometimes heartbreaking work. I have been there through the tears with my dear friend when a child just simply could not be saved.

I am in awe of April, because I see how hard she works, not only in her commitment to being successful and impactful in her career—which means doing all she can to ensure the health, wellness, wholeness, safety, support, and best education of her students—but also in her commitment as a wife and mom. Like many ambitious, working moms, it is an understatement to say she is juggling a lot, especially now that she has taken on this new challenge professionally. But with that awe, I sometimes worry, because lately I've noticed that when I, or others, ask her how she's doing, how things are going, or how she's feeling, April responds with, "Things feel tight." When I've pressed her on what she means by that, she repeats matter-of-factly, "Everything just feels tight."

Before we go on, let me say that if anything consistently feels "tight" for you physically—stress in your body, pain in your joints, stiffness in your neck, or, most urgent, tightness in your chest—you must get this checked out by a doctor immediately. Some "tightness" could be a sign that something is about to snap, give out, or give way. Think about a rubber band. You can only stretch it so far, right? You don't want to wait until that happens before you find out what's really going on.

Can you relate? That tight feeling, where your schedule is over-flowing with to-dos at work and at home and you don't feel like you have space to breathe? Where, even though you love what you do and of course you love your family, you could use a little cushion between the demands on your life? Are you tensing up right now as you read this, because it's triggering your own feelings of tightness that you contend with daily? If so, it's time for a change. Not only that, I want you to know that even though it may feel impossible right now, change *is* possible.

You must create space for support to come into your life, whatever that looks like for you. Learning to loosen your grip on the reins and let go of some of the control you perhaps think you need to maintain will allow you to relieve that dangerous tension.

During a video call—April was in Brooklyn and I was living in Sofia, Bulgaria, for a month—I ask April about the tightness she often mentions. She reflects: "It's funny, I remember you bringing that up to me before, too, and I do use the word 'tight.' I think that things feel tight when I'm on autopilot, and it feels like there's no room to breathe, have fun, think, feel. I'm realizing there's a difference between autopilot and routine."

She continues, "Autopilot is when you're going through your day, but you're not feeling and thinking. It's just like, I wake up, get the boys up, brush their teeth, get their hair done, breakfast. All that kind of stuff. Autopilot feels very tight because there's no room for anything to go wrong. Routine feels more like doing things, but being present while I'm doing them. I cannot breathe without routine."

For April, moving away from autopilot meant getting support in other areas of her life to create some space, which wasn't necessarily easy for her. "I'm Jamaican," she laughs. "There's a lot of respect that goes into hard work and doing things yourself. Growing up, I saw my mom do everything and balance everything on her own. She was a single mother but still had time to iron sheets on a Sunday. She cleaned houses on the side, and she had a full life. She did it all. I think that, for me, I felt that's what I was supposed to do."

April says she knew she had to make a change when she felt like things were starting to fall apart, and she could no longer hide it. "It was when my kids were young, and I just felt like a failure at work and a failure at home that I kind of embraced my incompetence to the point where it felt good to say that I didn't know, and it felt good to say that I needed help, and it felt good to *ask* for help. I got the feeling that people wanted to see me win. When I win, they're a part of that success, and they get to own that success and vice versa."

Part of that team that wants to see her win includes her husband, her mom, her sons' school, mommy support groups she belongs to, and our sister circle, which is crucial in her personal life. At work, it's her secretary, who supports her by asking her the same questions every single day. "I prioritize things in a notebook that I have," April explains. "If I don't prioritize, I know that things are going to fall apart. Sometimes I let my structure, like the system of my notebook, fall apart, so my secretary has the job of coming to me every morning and saying, 'Have you prioritized in your book?' If I say, 'Yes,' she says, 'Show me.' And I have to open my book and actually, like a four-year-old, show her my homework to prove that I've done it."

Whatever you have to do, whatever structure or fail-safe you have to put in place to create space for support in your life, do it. Now. While these tactics may sound extreme to some, they can be a matter of life and burnout for many of us. And burnout—defined by Webster's

Dictionary as "exhaustion of physical or emotional strength or motivation usually as a result of prolonged stress or frustration"—isn't just some trendy word people use to flaunt how busy they've been. It's real, sis.

Dawn Shedrick, CEO of JenTex Training & Consulting—a company that provides personal development training, continuing education webinars, and career development media for social workers—knows all about burnout. With a mission of supporting social workers and caretakers by making sure that they are as well cared for as the people they serve, Dawn has both supported others with avoiding burnout and had to learn how to do the same for herself as a woman who owns her own thriving business, cares for members of her family, and is an advocate for her community. "Burnout is a thing," she says bluntly during our call, citing occupational burnout, which is related to stress on the job, as one example. "There is considerable research that actually has been around for decades but now we, meaning a collective we—humanity-wise, not just in any particular sector—are starting to pay more attention to burnout and self-care."

Dawn's own struggles with burnout and with asking for support centered largely around her always being the go-to person—certainly within her business as the CEO, but also among family and friends who depend on her in different ways. And, although we may not always realize, no one needs more support than the "strong one" among us.

Have you ever seen those memes on social media that say: "Check on your strong friend"? Well, I posted a version of that on my personal Instagram account, @elaynefluker, that said: "Check on your strong friend. And if you are that strong friend, know that it's okay to say, 'I need help.' You deserve support."

Dawn said her personal shift from being the "strong one," doing it all, and carrying the world on her shoulders came when she let go of that false sense of independence and changed her beliefs about what it means to create space for support in her personal life and in her role as an entrepreneur and business owner.

"What I've come to understand is that creating the space for support is not just saying, 'Okay, let me open myself up to support,'" she says. "It is about reflecting on the sociocultural influences of those beliefs—such as family legacies of 'if you want it done right, do it yourself,' and being the oldest child, to name a few—and dismantling them because they have held me back from asking for and receiving support throughout my entrepreneurial journey."

Beliefs. They are powerful forces, but they are not necessarily the truth. They are what we *believe* to be true. Sometimes we forget this. Think about the belief of some in our world today that we are, as human beings, more different than we are the same. Think of how much hatred, dysfunction, strife, and suffering this belief causes us around the world. Think about your own beliefs that may have you convinced that you are not worthy of your success, or that you have something to prove in order to stay successful, or that you have to be the straight-A student, the one who always gets the proverbial gold star, the one on whom people depend. Or the belief that, God forbid, if you were to ask for support, no one would show up for you.

This is something that Dawn had to contend with in changing her beliefs not only around support, but around her own identity as it related to support. She realized that oftentimes, while she was struggling to do something alone and support everyone else around her—believing that if she didn't do it, it wouldn't get done—support for her was actually there waiting in the wings for her to notice.

"I'm a social worker," she says. "That is [work] defined by helping others. I'm [also] a caretaker to more than one family member. Those aren't necessarily albatrosses in my life, but I've realized that I kind of just fell in alignment with being the caretaker for everyone else.

"Once I stepped into that consciousness and started to explore, 'Well, what does that really mean for me? What have I created as a result of that identity?'" she says, "That is how I have been able to let go of it as a primary identity and be much more open to seeking support."

Dawn says one of the identities she had to let go of was thinking she was the only one who could solve fill-in-the-blank problems. When she did, her awareness of the abundance of support around her became heightened. Support was finally able to come out from the wings and join her. She realized there were people who had been offering her support or who had been there that she didn't even need to ask. "Sometimes I did receive it, but a lot of times I didn't," she confesses.

Have you ever had moments when you feel like you're carrying your world (your partner, your kids, your family, your friends, your colleagues, your clients, your business, etc.) on your shoulders and that no one ever shows up to support you? Have you ever paused during those moments to examine that belief and consider that maybe, just maybe, you're not creating space for those people to show up for you? Could it be that you have had your blinders on for years, and you've been so hyper-focused on solving the issue on your own that you haven't noticed those on your left and on your right who are just waiting for you to tag them in so they can unload some of that weight you've been carrying and lift you up? Have you made the ask? Pause for a moment and give that some thought now.

If you realize you've been that person, don't beat yourself up. Many of us as ambitious and "busy" women have been there: frustrated and feeling like, "F—it, I'll do it," when it comes to problem solving, no matter what that problem is. We believe we're the only one who can handle it. And some of us take pride in this belief, being the martyr for the cause unnecessarily just so we feel needed. But again, don't beat yourself up. Instead, open yourself up. Take a break from being the "strong one," and instead let yourself be a vessel for receiving support.

Dawn says that taking this important step meant she had to go deep and do what she calls some "unlearning." What's unlearning? It goes back to dismantling and discarding those limiting beliefs that hold you back. "I think in some instances you have to unlearn what you currently believe in order to learn something new," she tells me after a long pause to think about the concept. "I've been connecting with women entrepreneurs who themselves have embraced [unlearning] in the same way. *What are those habits? What are those beliefs I have that are not working? How can I unlearn them and give myself permission to unlearn them—give myself permission for the change?*"

TAKE ACTION:
SAY "YES!"

No one falls victim to "I Got It!" Syndrome more than the strong ones. But today you're going to change that. I want you to commit to saying "yes" to allowing support in your life at least one time every single day over the next seven days starting today. If no one offers support to you during one of those days, you get to find a way to ask for it. It can be something small like asking your coworker to hold your coffee while you find something in your bag or asking a stranger for directions you don't really need. The answer, or the response to your request, doesn't matter, and neither does the result of the support you say "yes" to and receive. It's about you shifting your mindset around receiving help by taking these small actions consistently and getting into the habit of asking for and accepting support from genuine people who can or do offer it to you.

At the end of each night, grab your journal and write down how you asked for or accepted support that day and how you felt about it. The point is, have fun with it. At first, it may feel awkward for you, maybe even a little scary. Eventually, you'll likely notice it will become easier, as do most things with practice. After a week, I invite you to keep it going. Soon a week will be a month, a month will be two, and you will have developed this healthy new habit.

You can learn how to unravel your limiting beliefs about support and stop feeling obligated to be the "strong one." Just give yourself permission. And practice.

SECTION TWO

Ask Empowering Questions

"When we're living a question, we're living
in that state of creativity and curiosity and
openness. It's such a bigger, broader view of
life, and it makes it a lot easier to navigate those
inevitable ups and downs and obstacles."

—Patricia Moreno,
creator of intenSati

7

Live the Question

In addition to giving ourselves permission to unlearn the behaviors, habits, and beliefs that no longer serve us and to choose to be receptive to support, we also have to give ourselves permission to not know all the answers. And for unapologetically ambitious women, who are leaders in our companies or founders of our businesses, knowing the answers—or knowing how to find the answers—is not only how we make the big bucks, it's also how we have come to hold these positions. As entrepreneur Dawn Shedrick says, it is a part of our identity. For moms and caretakers, too. People turn to you for the answers because you are a problem solver. You are a woman who gets shit done.

But here's the thing: sometimes you gotta be okay with not knowing. You have to get comfortable allowing yourself to be in that space in between the answers and the certainty and the periods of your life when you believe you have everything figured out.

You have to learn how to live the question.

When I first heard this phrase, *live the question*, it was a humid day in August 2016. I was sitting at a tiny wooden desk that was previously owned by my Grandma Minnie in the 1930s, and I was facing a bright yellow wall, hunched over a microphone, in the spare room of my apartment on the top floor of a brownstone in Brooklyn, New York. I was just a few episodes into my new podcast for women entrepreneurs called *Support is Sexy*, and I was on a Skype call interviewing a woman named Patricia Moreno, who created a popular, transformative workout called intenSati. I learned about Patricia through a mutual friend, Lucy Osborne, with whom I was in a mastermind group at the time. Lucy invited us all to one of Patricia's classes at a store in Manhattan's West Village, and I fell in love with intenSati, the concept, the workout, and its intention that day. But when I interviewed Patricia for my podcast, she gave me a gift that keeps on giving several years later: live the question.

During our interview, Patricia told me about the period of her life—before intenSati took shape as the powerful movement it is today—when she wasn't exactly sure what she was going to create, but she had an idea of what it could be. She knew she wanted to create a different kind of workout routine, but there was something else. Something for her was missing, and she wasn't sure what that something was.

Instead of desperately searching high and low, trying to find the answer to what was missing (which, hello, that's what I would have done and what I usually obsessed about doing until I learned this incredible gem from her), she allowed herself to live the question. The empowering question. So, as she told me during our interview, the question wasn't "Why am I such an asshole?" just because she couldn't immediately figure out the answers. The question was steeped in the acknowledgment that she was smart and a good person and someone who was willing to work hard. So, she asked the Universe: "What am I missing?" And then, she created space for the answer to show up. Each day, she chose to live the question.

The first part of the answer to Patricia's question came in Fiji during a retreat, where spiritual teacher Deepak Chopra spoke about why our identities must align with our purpose; otherwise, we will never be able to stick to whatever goal we are trying to achieve. As she thought about this while in the shower later that day, she says she had a light-bulb moment about the question she was living. If your identity is "I am fat," you will always identify as fat, even if you lose weight, she thought. As a result, you'll eventually return to the way you identify.

Patricia, who says she had personally struggled with her own weight since childhood—reaching 180 pounds as a preteen—realized that if she wanted to help people stick to healthy routines and make lasting change, she had to help them shift their identity around their body image, and that she could do so by combining powerful fitness movements with affirming statements. The next part of the answer to the question she was living came to her while walking along the beach during yet another retreat, where she realized she could create the practice that allowed people to embody their affirmations holistically, making it easier for them to commit to this new lifestyle. As a result, intenSati was born.

When it comes to episodes of the *Support is Sexy* podcast, I refuse to say I have favorites (because who wants to pick one of their kids as the one they like best, right?). But I do cite Patricia's episode (episode twenty-six out of more than seven hundred as of the writing of this book) as one that had the most lasting impact on me, my mindset, and how I approach uncertainty, which can often be unnerving. I have learned to live the question and let the answers come to me.

Actually, true confession: I am still learning how to live the question. It takes practice and requires a mindset shift around what not knowing the answers says about you and how powerful, smart, capable, and worthy you are. You have to let that go. Living the question does not cripple you. On the contrary, it allows you to tap into something very powerful: your curiosity. And curious people who ask empowering, thoughtful, and simply *better* questions tend to come up with better answers. Each time I commit to that practice, the answer shows up in the most unexpected places and at the perfect times without fail.

"Everything we are feeling is a result of how we're using our minds," Patricia tells me as I gush over the impact of our conversation from years ago during our more recent video call to discuss the idea of living the question for this book. "When we ask questions, our brain is constantly seeking answers. If we're asking better questions, we're gonna get better answers. When we're willing to just live in this state of curiosity and openness, then it opens our mind to be looking for things that are outside of the normal realm of perception."

This means letting go of what you think you know and going from know-it-all (yes, you!) to what Patricia calls a "curious architect."

"When we're living a question, we're living in that state of creativity and curiosity and openness," she says. "It's such a bigger, broader view of life, and it makes it a lot easier to navigate those inevitable ups and downs and obstacles."

Patricia says living the question also frees us from tying our identities to our failures and even to our successes. Neither of those define us, unless we allow them to. "We don't have to think of failures as an identity or something that's taking a little bit of time [to figure out] as, 'There's something wrong with me.'" Living the question, she says, "leads us into living a life that is more fun, more playful, more open, more curious, and I think it, at least in my experience, tends to lead me to being kinder to myself."

Do you find that you're tough on yourself, maybe even mean to yourself, just because you don't know all the answers, because you can't quickly solve the problem, because whatever you thought was going to work out a certain way didn't work out that way or meet your expectations? Have you ever blamed yourself for getting something wrong, or demeaned yourself because you felt like you should've known better? Instead of banging your head against the wall trying to determine the answer or figure out what you did "wrong," living the question allows you to be gentle with yourself, to give yourself permission to learn and grow, to show yourself a little bit of grace—a grace you absolutely deserve.

We all have moments of not knowing. Our willingness to live the question is what separates those who spiral into despair, and possibly into depression when we don't know the answers, from those who embrace not knowing as a chance to be curious architects. And, beyond that, to trust that the answer—the support—will show up for you. The Universe wants you to prosper, sis.

The thing is, you have to believe that this is true, and not depend solely on your own understanding to solve every problem or overcome every obstacle that comes your way. "When I'm asking the question, I'm using my conscious mind, my limited mind, to tap into a more all-knowing mind, and in that way it's kind of an act of humility," Patricia says. "When you're asking the question, you're asking for help. It's humbling to ask for help and the ego says, 'You should know this already,' or 'You should be better than this.'"

Instead of allowing your ego to control you and close you off to the possibilities of what living the question could bring into your life, Patricia says surrender to that "state of openness."

When I ask her what stops some of us, as ambitious women and leaders, from wanting to surrender or feel like we've given up, she doesn't talk about how courageous and strong and independent we are for holding our ground; she actually cites what she calls an *epidemic of fear.* Fear of not appearing perfect and pulled together to the outside world, which can lead to intense stress.

"There's a lot of stress to look right, make more, do more, and have more, and we have to really remember, at all costs, that stress is never going to get you where you want to go," she says.

When you surrender, you make a conscious decision to release that negative thinking. Patricia says meditation is one powerful way to connect to that feeling of surrender and to open yourself up to the answers that will come from living the question.

A phrase she uses that I love and immediately adopted when she said it, is: "I surrender all fear, and faith reappears."

In times of fear, stress, chaos, or anxiety, when you need to get centered and grounded, try repeating this phrase quietly to yourself as many times as you need to until you feel yourself relax, until your breathing slows, until you create some space for clarity. Before that big meeting, before and after that difficult conversation, as you walk down a crowded street, or as you simply sit quietly by yourself at home. Even as a whisper, it is so powerful:

I surrender all fear and faith reappears.
I surrender all fear and faith reappears.
I surrender all fear and faith reappears.

Says Patricia: "When we say, 'Okay, I'm going to surrender this fear. I'm going to understand that this is an outcome. This fear, this anxiety, this feeling of unworthiness, this feeling of lack, this feeling of limitation, it's an outcome that I have the power to navigate, to interrupt, to surrender, and to choose another response.' I think it's super important that we learn to master ourselves in this way, because otherwise we're just working from the same limitations that got us to the outcomes that we're living today."

TAKE ACTION:
MEDITATE ON IT

If meditation is new for you, or even if you meditate regularly, I've created a guided mindfulness meditation that you can download and listen to at any time to help you get re-centered, surrender the fear, and live the question in an empowering way. Go to elaynefluker.com to download it now.

8

Learn the Language of the Ask

As Patricia Moreno explains, fear, shame, and our own limiting beliefs often keep us, as ambitious women, from living the question, being vulnerable, embracing our curiosity, and admitting—even if just to ourselves at first—that we don't have all the answers and that we need support.

But for some women, the hesitancy to live the question, ask for support, and embrace vulnerability may be compounded by something deeply ingrained in us and even more difficult to overcome than fear or embarrassment. It may be related to our cultural history and what we've been taught about the privilege of asking.

In her article "Closed Mouths Don't Get Fed: Black Women and the Language of the Ask," Kathryn Finney—serial entrepreneur, founder and former CEO of digitalundivided, named by *Forbes* as one of "America's Top 50 Women in Tech," and a staunch advocate for women of color entrepreneurs—shares why she believes Black women, especially, don't request the support they often desperately need.

Kathryn writes:

> Imagine being hurt or even killed for asking for your most basic rights as an American. The right to the pursuit of happiness. The right to liberty. The right to life.
>
> What happens then? You stop being vulnerable. You stop dreaming.
>
> You stop asking.
>
> It's a privileged position to think that if you ask someone for something, anything, that you will, in fact, receive it. That you, as a living, breathing human have a right to dream and to believe. As a result, the entire concept of dreaming becomes a radical act.
>
> The language of the "ask" is new to my community of women. From a very early age, we're told by our parents and our community, verbally and through social cues, to "stop asking." When we respond to the denial by crying, we're told, "I'll give you something to cry about," a strikingly common statement among our parents.[1]

Kathryn goes on to explain that for many Black Americans of a previous generation, especially those who lived through the harsh, dehumanizing racism, discrimination, and brutal violence during the Jim Crow era and the civil rights movement, tempering your desires was a survival mechanism. You didn't ask because you didn't want to end up disappointed, and, likewise, you didn't want your children to be disappointed, or, even worse, you didn't want them to get hurt or killed. That was the reality.

It's difficult to reconcile asking—and having the right to ask and the belief that you will receive—when you were an individual who didn't have permission for simple acts like sitting at the same lunch counter and eating a sandwich next to someone who is white, or sitting in whichever seat is empty on a public bus after a long day of work, or, as my mother—an Alabama native—told me, trying on shoes in the store before buying them, which was prohibited because the storekeeper didn't want them back after your feet had been in them just because you were Black. You guessed your size, you got your shoes, and you got the hell out of there as fast as you could, she told me. As a result, she and her siblings often ended up with shoes that didn't fit properly and that hurt their feet as they walked those dirt roads. But they wouldn't dare ask for anything different.

This historical context around "the ask" is why many Black women have learned to, as Kathryn says, "swallow their pain," and not ask for support. We didn't grow up witnessing or experiencing what it was like to ask and to expect to receive. In fact, no matter what our socioeconomic status, many of us were told that you have to work twice as hard to be considered half as good as your white counterparts. We saw what it was like to sacrifice, and in some cases to suffer, in silence to get ahead or merely to survive.

Yet, remarkably, many Black women still strive for high levels of success today despite that historical pain. And when we do achieve that success, it doesn't mean that the pain goes away. Instead we teeter precariously between success and the desperate need for love and support while wearing a mask that portrays us as "strong" to the outside world. We endure the daily microaggressions based on our race and gender at the office in order to advance our careers, the overt aggressions in government policies that affect our bodies and our rights as women, the inequalities in pay and promotions even though we may be equally or even more qualified for the job, and the feelings of disregard from the lack of support we sometimes feel within our own communities. As a result of these repressed feelings, we often end up angry—which compounds our resistance to asking for support with yet another complex we have to contend with: the "angry Black woman" narrative.

"We're really angry, and rightfully so!" Kathryn asserts during our call to discuss her article and the language of the ask. "We don't know how to process it because we're not given the space to process it. We don't know where to place the emotions because we're told to not have any. If you're told to not have any emotions, when you feel angry you have no idea what to do with it.

"You don't want to be the 'angry black woman'—even though you have the right to be angry because no one gave you the space to be angry and the space to also transcend that anger."

The issue is, swallowing this pain and this anger is like swallowing poison. We end up sick and suffering while, again, presenting as strong. This is especially true for "accomplished" women in the community. The more successful and admired you appear to everyone else, the less they believe you need support or therapy that could help you work through these complicated emotions. And the less likely you are to ask. There is still a nasty, unfortunate stigma attached to the idea of therapy—and mental illness—among many in the Black community. Fortunately, we have started to see public figures speaking openly about their own experiences or the experiences of their loved ones when it comes to mental health challenges. Actress Taraji P. Henson, for example, has shared that her son struggled with mental health after his father was murdered in 2003, and that her father, who died in 2005, also had mental health challenges. Henson opened The Boris Lawrence Henson Foundation to, according to their website at borislhensonfoundation.org, "eradicate the stigma around mental health issues in The African-American community." Henson told

Variety magazine that she felt it was important that her face be attached to the foundation, which is named in honor of her father—a Vietnam War veteran—so people see that, yes, even celebrities like her have real problems and seek therapy as well.[2]

And for women like Kathryn, therapy has been crucial in helping her get to her position of success and stay there. "I can tell you, as a Black woman, it's taken me many years of therapy to be able to get to this point, and even then I still fully don't allow my husband to do things for me, or ask for help and say, 'You know what? I need space right now,' or, 'Mommy needs a half a day,'" Kathryn tells me when I ask how she has become comfortable with asking for support.

"I'm very open about it, and I can tell when it makes people really uncomfortable because someone like me is not supposed to have been someone who has gone through years of therapy, because of my success, because of the perception. People are like, 'Oh, you seem pretty put together.' I'm like, 'That's because I went to years of therapy.'"

Whatever your cultural background, upbringing, education, or socioeconomics, as a woman, you have to realize that therapy, coaching, counseling, and asking for support—whether it's for your personal life, your professional life, or even your dating life—are not signs of weakness. Just as expressing your vulnerability—your humanity—is not weakness or neediness. It is, in fact, empowering, if you choose to adjust your mindset and view it that way.

As Dr. Brené Brown, best-selling author and researcher of vulnerability, empathy, and shame, said in her TED talk, "Listening to Shame," it is dangerous to view vulnerability as a sign of weakness. On the contrary, she says, it is the greatest indicator of our courage.[3]

Kathryn Finney had to learn how to flex her own vulnerability muscle when she first had her son, who, as I am writing this book, is three years old. As a celebrated entrepreneur building a disruptive technology company while caring for her growing family, she reached a point where she felt like things were slipping. And it was her mom who stepped in to help.

"When we first moved to Atlanta, I was not winning by any stretch of the imagination," Kathryn shares candidly. "I wasn't winning professionally. I wasn't winning personally. Things were not good. Everything was coming at me at once, and I was not doing well. I remember I had this conversation with my mother. I was really upset, and she said to me, 'Do you need me to come?' I thought she was going to come for like an hour. She said, 'No, do you need me to move to Atlanta to help you?' I was like, 'Yeah, I do. I really do. Yes, I need your help. I need you to come.'

"That, to me, was a moment of vulnerability, and that was a moment of me admitting that I couldn't do what I needed to do and that I needed help. My mother saying, 'You ask and I'm going to answer, and this is how I can help,' was really a game changer. I don't think [my former company], digitalundivided, would be where it is if my mother didn't come and help. I know it wouldn't have been."

Moving beyond our cultural hang-ups around support is possible, but acknowledging them, untangling them, and working through them are imperative steps to getting through to the other side, as is our commitment to doing things differently than we may have been taught or conditioned. Otherwise, your growth, your success, and your wellness will always be stunted by the perception that support is only for a privileged group of people, that you're "too strong" to ask, or that asking says something negative about who you are. Again, no matter your background, economic status, or your cultural history, know that *you* deserve support, whatever that looks like for you. Embrace the idea that authentic vulnerability is a sign of strength. Learn the language of the ask. And practice it until you become fluent.

TAKE ACTION:
KNOW WHAT IT MEANS TO
BE VULNERABLE AND SAFE

Being vulnerable takes courage. Being vulnerable takes practice. Being vulnerable also takes trust—trust that you're within a safe space. Sharing your inner thoughts, feelings, desires, insecurities, and everything else should only be done in spaces where you are aware of your surroundings. This doesn't mean that you can control the environment, but are you aware of the environment?

For example, if you're sharing details about a traumatic experience for the first time, are you doing so in a space that will honor you and your experience? Are you in a space where you feel supported? Are you in a space where, if there is any pushback, you trust that the dialogue will be respectful, productive, and edifying, even if an agreement is not met?

And if you're sharing in an anything-goes public space, such as social media (or where something you say may be broadcast on social media, such as a conference), are you prepared for what may follow—which, unfortunately, may not always be as supportive as we'd hope? I believe many of the people who attack others on social media are, themselves, in some kind of pain that they have not dealt with or recognized, so they hide behind their keyboards and unleash their anger on others as an outlet. Hurt people hurt people. Yet, while we may understand this, it doesn't sting any less when you're on the receiving end of a venomous attack.

When practicing vulnerability, only you can be the judge of what feels safe for you, but here are some things I want you to consider:

1. It's okay to share your scars and not your wounds. Sometimes, in the era of social media, we are quick to want to share what's going on in our lives in the moment. But when you're in the thick of a difficult situation, consider if it would be best to share your wounds within a safe space and in an environment that may offer you some healing (such as with a trusted counselor or therapist). Then share the scars—which are the result of that wound healing—when the time is right. Just because you're keeping something private doesn't mean you're keeping it a secret. You have every right to your privacy.

And, as a leader, the public—meaning your colleagues, your employees, your audience, or your fans and followers—may not be prepared to handle the extent of your wounds, especially if you're someone people admire. This doesn't mean that they don't realize that you hurt just as other humans hurt. And this does not mean you don't have a right to your emotions or your pain. But in choosing to share your scars instead, you can share your experience (the wound) and how you went about healing it and addressing it (the scar) as well as the lessons you learned from that time in your life in a way that not only offers hope to others, but allows you to celebrate how you overcame it.

2. Know that everybody can't come. You might want the safe space to be within your family. You might want that safe space to be within your marriage or relationship. You might want the safe space to be between you and your girlfriends. The unfortunate truth is, sometimes, it just isn't. This doesn't mean that the people in your life are bad or uncaring or unloving people. It simply means they may not be able to handle what you want or need to share. Perhaps they have their own trauma or challenges they're contending with, perhaps conflict makes them uncomfortable, perhaps they just don't want to deal. Again, this doesn't make them bad people, and if we try to force people in our lives to handle our vulnerability when they don't have the capacity to do so, we can often make them out to be bad or insensitive. Instead, realize that everybody can't come. When it comes to your healing, your evolution, your journey, you may have to go partway without the people who are otherwise by your side, but you still don't have to do it alone. There are plenty of other ways for you to find support. Try a trusted coach, a mentor, or a counselor. But don't use your family or friends as an excuse. This is about your health and well-being.

3. Find your vulnerability warriors. Take out your journal and use this time to write down three people you can depend on for support to be what I call your vulnerability warriors. These are individuals who are courageous enough to share with you, and loving enough to not judge when you share with them. Who can you trust to be objective listeners, who will give you thoughtful, honest feedback? These can be people you pay or people you already have in your life. But it must be someone. Don't know anyone personally? Again, make it a priority to find a coach, therapist, a psychiatrist, a counselor, a mentor, or a support group. Do your research and write down three groups or organizations that you're going to connect with in the next seven days that could provide you with a safe space for sharing and being vulnerable. As psychologist Kongit Farrell says, you have to curate your safe environment.

If, for any reason, it is urgent that you share or ask for help—for example, if you are being physically or verbally abused, if you are being harassed, or if you are being threatened in any way—share now. Find someone you trust and ask for help. Tell him or her that you urgently need help. Your physical and mental safety are of the utmost importance. Take care of you.

9

Remove Your Mask

I n that 2012 TED talk (see Chapter 8), "Listening to Shame," Dr. Brené Brown says that what shame looks like for most women is doing it all perfectly, and never letting 'em see you sweat while you're doing it.[1] For some successful women, the idea of being vulnerable isn't just something to avoid by not asking for support or letting you see us sweat, we also try to make sure that you never glimpse that side of us by wearing "the mask."

The mask is that facade you hide behind in order to conceal your true feelings and who you really are from the outside world. And that mask might look different for every woman. It could be the mask of the fiercely "independent" woman, or the emotionless CEO, or the woman who "has it all," or the woman who is the perfect mom, or the woman who is the constant contrarian, or the woman who is an unwavering people pleaser. In each case, the mask supports a false narrative about what you're really feeling, experiencing, or needing in the moment. And when you've been wearing that mask for too long, it could cause you to end up living somewhat of a double life: appearing one way on the outside while suffering on the inside. Eventually, however, it will become much too heavy to bear, and, ironically, though you may have been using that mask to hold up your image, it could be just the thing that brings you down.

Lisa Brown Alexander, CEO of Nonprofit HR—a Washington, DC–based human resources firm focused exclusively on the social impact sector—and author of the book *Strong on the Outside, Dying on the Inside*, will never forget the moment, fifteen years ago, when she realized she could no longer bear the weight of the mask she had chosen to wear for so many years. Lisa says she was at the height of her career, but also experiencing the height of her depression. Because, you see, your mask isn't just there for you to hide behind when things are not going well. Sometimes things are going *so* well in some areas of your life that you want to make sure—at all costs—that it continues to appear perfect to everyone in your world. At her tipping point, however, Lisa's perfect mask was about to crack, and her world was about to crumble if she didn't get support.

"It was a very distinct moment, and even to this day I remember it," Lisa tells me as I chat with her while I am in Marrakech, Morocco, and she is on the road heading home from DC. "My husband and I were on vacation, on a cruise, and I should have been happy and enjoying the sunshine. Instead, I wasn't. I was just desperate for air and desperate to get better. I remember going to the top of the ship, sitting in the sun—and feeling very cold even though the sun was blazing—and just begging God for my life back."

Lisa, whose company, Nonprofit HR, was thriving at the time, was beyond stressed. She was struggling to still show up as the powerful, pulled-together CEO, who has a beautiful family and all the other items on her dream-life wish list ticked off, while deep down she was suffering in silence. "I was just exhausted from feeling bad and disconnected," she says. "I came back from that trip with a very strong resolve to get help. I got the support of a psychologist and therapist, and she talked me out of that hole."

That hole, for Lisa, was the result of her addiction to what she calls her "drug of choice"—work and success—and it had become a way of self-medicating from the pain and unhappiness that she felt but couldn't communicate. The pressure to "look the part, act the part, and walk the part" was very real, and Lisa was staying in line. She walked that line—and swallowed that pain—for five years.

"It becomes a self-fulfilling prophecy when other people see you working really hard, not knowing that you're medicating, but they're like, 'Oh, give it to Susan, give it to Shanika,'" she says. "And you take it on because of a multitude of reasons, the least of which is it helps to numb the pain, but it also fulfills your desire to meet the expectation that people have of you or exceed it in some instances."

On top of that, Lisa, a mother of three, was dealing with "mommy guilt" and trying to manage being present for the office while also being present for her three children because, as an ambitious mommy, those worlds somehow have to coexist. "It's not that separate, and our lives are intertwined," Lisa says when I ask her if, as a mom, she ever felt pressured to choose one over the other. "It's never that perfect and that segregated. It's fluid and it's organic, and things can change at a moment's notice, which causes you to have to recalibrate everything else in the time you spend. So, it's an ongoing struggle. Do you finish that report, or do you go sit on your child's bed and have a conversation about their day before they go to sleep? You know what I mean? It's tough," she says.

Lisa says her mask was made even heavier by the fact that she is a woman of faith—and as a devoted Christian woman, she was raised to believe that prayer, alone, was the only answer.

"That compounds the tendency that we have to keep it to ourselves," she says of her own experience. Lisa decided she needed "both prayer and partnership by way of a mental health professional," and she had to set aside whatever criticisms others might have about her getting that support. "I was desperate at that point, and I knew I had to save myself from myself."

What's the mask that you're wearing in your life? Is it one you feel you have to wear in order to appear strong to your loved ones at home or to get ahead at the office? Is it one you're protecting because of your faith? Or is it one you're wearing because, as Lisa says, you've "assigned it" to yourself in order to present some level of perfection? And how deep are the wounds that might be buried beneath that mask? At what point will you decide enough is enough and have the courage to be real about who you are, where you are, and what you're feeling?

This isn't to say that, as I mentioned earlier, you have to reveal your deepest secrets to everyone you meet, and it's definitely not to say that you should open up painful wounds in spaces that don't feel safe to you. You can, however, decide today that you want to start to chip away at your mask and discover what's beneath with the help of a supportive guide—a coach, a therapist, a psychiatrist, a spiritual teacher, a mentor—whatever feels right for you at this time. The reasons you, even as a successful woman, choose to wear your mask may surprise you.

That's the trouble with the mask, though. It allows you to hide in so many different areas of your life and to get comfortable doing so—areas you may not have even considered (that's why a guide is a good idea to help you get a different perspective). When you get used to throwing your mask on so often (or maybe never taking it off), you start to lose yourself, and then you may start to resent yourself and possibly resent everything and everyone around you, which can lead you to feel unfulfilled, isolated, and depressed. No matter how successful you are, if you don't make a change, stress will build and things will fall apart. You can't use the mask to run from yourself forever because, as the saying goes, no matter where you go, there you are.

I know I certainly was surprised when I discovered some of the reasons I wear my own mask. Mine is painted in brightly colored "independence." (I was, after all, the queen of "I Got It!" Syndrome at one point in my life.) Support, as I have shared, used to make me feel weak, less than perfect, way too vulnerable, and, as Brené Brown says, ashamed. But this perception didn't only impact why I didn't know how to ask for what I needed as a teenager, or the way I often worked myself to the bone all alone to be successful as an adult. It also comes into play in my romantic relationships, or lack thereof.

See, while some women put on the mask to prove how capable they are at work or in their businesses, I realized that I had a habit of using my career as my drug of choice and wore my mask as an excuse to avoid intimate relationships because "I'm just too busy." Instead, I chose to remain independent—in other words, alone. Now, there's nothing wrong with choosing to be single, but honestly, that's not what I really wanted. The real reason behind my mask was fear of disappointment, trust issues after one too many adulterous partners, and not wanting to put my time and energy into something that makes me so vulnerable when I don't have control over the outcome—namely, whether my heart gets broken. So, for years, I decided not to make room for romance in my life. That's real talk.

It took years of chipping away at my mask of independence for me to open myself up to love. I finally admitted to myself that, as much as I am ambitious and as much as I do care about the success and the impact of my business, I do want love, I do want a partnership, I do want someone who's there to be a witness to this thing called life with me. I want someone who encourages me to feel comfortable being my vulnerable, authentic self—which, sometimes, isn't the pulled-together, powerful woman everyone else sees in public. And, above all, I finally realized that I deserve that.

Getting to this point took work, though. Work and, for me, getting away from my routine, busy life for a while. In 2018, I did just that. For five months, from July through December, I traveled with a company called Remote Year to five countries with a group of about thirty amazing individuals from all parts of the world, who are now like family to me. Through Spain, Bulgaria, South Africa, Prague (Czech Republic), and Morocco, we lived and worked in each country for a month and had to learn our way around, experience the culture, explore the unknown, and push ourselves outside of our comfort zones. Though I have always had a serious wanderlust, I had never done anything like that before—relinquishing control of my itinerary, my accommodations, where I worked, and with whom I traveled. The experience changed my life.

The change happened not only because I had to navigate living and working remotely in a new country each month—not to mention, I was writing the first draft of this book the entire time. I also had to push myself to connect with this group of individuals and try things I had never done, from unique foods to unforgettable activities, like hiking South Africa's Lion's Head mountain at four o'clock in the morning, going shark diving with great whites, strolling through the streets of Soweto, taking a two-day jaunt to another country (from Bulgaria to Greece and back), and even running in a half marathon through a breathtaking vineyard in Cape Town, South Africa. I credit Remote Year with teaching me how to open myself up to the unknown, let loose, go with the flow, and be okay with a little uncertainty. Most important, the experience taught me to make time for fun. In fact, I learned the importance of adding fun to my calendar. To this day, I have "Have fun" scheduled in as standing appointments.

The experience also taught me something else. I wanted a partner, someone to return to at home. And this time, when I said it, I meant it.

To be clear, I have always said I wanted to be with someone. I have what I call a "vision recording" that I've been doing since 2015. Essentially it is a recording of me reading out my vision and desires for my life with affirming "I am" statements that I first write down in my journal. Studies show that nothing is more powerful in your mind than your own voice, whether that voice is encouraging or discouraging. This is why it's important to be conscious of how we speak to ourselves, even silently. Your words, your internal dialogue, your negative self-talk, and your thoughts have immense power in how you move through your life and what you believe.

To this day, I listen to my vision recording each morning. I've updated it a couple times over the years, and within each recording, there was always a part about relationships and the kind of partner I desired. I will admit to you here and now that, for years, I said it (and each day I listened to it) but I didn't mean it. I never made room for it. So, you know what? It never happened.

Things changed, however, during my final month of Remote Year in December. I was staying at the exquisite Jnane Tamsna boutique hotel in Marrakech, Morocco, which is owned by Meryanne Loum-Martin—an extraordinary visionary who is credited with pioneering the boutique hotel industry in Marrakech decades ago by welcoming international guests into her family's private home and creating unforgettable experiences for them. I had dreamed about interviewing Meryanne ever since seeing her—a stunningly beautiful, elegant, silver-haired Black French woman featured on Essence.com just a few months before I left for my trip. My goal was to interview her for the *Support is Sexy* podcast, which I did, but I never, ever imagined I would conduct the interview in person while tucked away at her fabulous hotel. Actually, Meryanne, whom I had the pleasure of getting to know well during my visit, invited me to extend my stay and take one of the rooms in her breathtaking home, which is on the hotel grounds. The experience was surreal, and I was honored. One afternoon, while sitting in the lush garden of Jnane Tamsna, I wrote out my latest vision. And then, with birds singing joyfully in the background, I hit record on my phone to record that vision.

Just like before, within this vision, I outlined the type of man with whom I wanted to develop a loving, passionate, joyful, supportive relationship. I shared where I wanted us to live, the type of house we would share, and the family I wanted to create with him. I gave details about the type of person he would be and how we supported each other and made each other better people and better entrepreneurs. I said it all. And this time, I meant it. I was finally ready to remove my mask and make room for true love.

I recorded that vision on December 20, 2018, in the garden of Jnane Tamsna hotel in Marrakech, Morocco. I returned to Atlanta, Georgia, to spend the holidays with my parents on December 25, and on the long flight back I decided that I was finally going to give myself a chance to settle here and not worry about hurrying back to New York. I was going to open myself up to the possibilities in Atlanta. On December 26, I headed to the local gym so I could join and continue the active lifestyle that I had picked up during Remote Year. And on December 26, at that gym, I met someone, and we had a whirlwind romance for almost a year. Though that relationship amicably ended, I recognize that the only way I was able to see that opportunity for love was by removing my mask, and I'm excited about what love will bring next.

Since removing her mask, Lisa says her life has also gone in a new direction. She says she knows how to check herself when she feels like she is slipping into that state of mind where work is overwhelming and she is beginning to reach for her mask again.

"I listen," she says. "I listen to my spirit and my mind and the Holy Spirit, quite honestly, telling me, 'You know what? You have to slow down.' And if I start to feel disappointed or sad . . . I have a conversation with myself that says, 'You can't go back to that place. So, you need to eradicate anything that is contributing to how you're feeling, whether it's a person, or a place, or a thing. Just get it out. Cut it off so that you can get back to a better place.'"

Instead of self-medicating with work, Lisa has learned to prioritize self-care—so much so that she and her husband opened a new wellness retreat in Maryland called Wellspring Manor & Spa, a place for people to escape from the hustle and bustle of life and find much-needed rest and rejuvenation. The new business, she says, reflects how she recharged her own life. "This has probably been one of the best times of my life in terms of self-fulfillment," she happily shares. "I won't say 'balance,' because I don't think I've mastered it yet; but certainly career and self-fulfillment."

TAKE ACTION:
BE YOURSELF

When it comes to taking off your own mask, Lisa Brown Alexander offers these three pieces of advice to get you started:

1. Turn it off. "The first thing is to give yourself permission to not be on all the time. Give yourself permission to step back and step away. Life will continue even when you take a moment for yourself. The world will not stop. We tell ourselves that, 'Everybody needs me. I need to be here for so and so, Mooky and Ray Ray and mama and them.' Sometimes you just need to take care of *you*. So, give yourself permission to do that. It's okay. Your children will be okay for a couple days if you take care of you. And why not take care of you so that you can continue to take care of them? If you have the assignment of caregiver in your family, whether it's immediate or extended, you need to recharge so that you can continue in the role that you have, and continue in a way that's effective and affirming."

2. Do something intentional. "Once you give yourself permission, be intentional about addressing your pain. Pick up the phone and call a therapist, make an appointment, go on vacation. Do something specific to break from the kind of pattern that you've found yourself in. Do something, do it on purpose."

3. Tap into a higher power. "Keep your ear and your spirit open to God's voice. God is going to tell you. If you stay open, He will tell you that you need a break, you need to slow down, you need to stop. You have to listen and you have to obey. Listen to spirit."

10

Reinvent with Support

Choosing to rid ourselves of our masks is one thing, but what about those moments when you are forced to reveal the real you, confront your vulnerabilities, and perhaps let go of something you didn't even realize was a mask?

Such was the challenge for legendary magazine editor Lesley Jane Seymour when she learned that *More* magazine—where she was editor-in-chief at the time—was folding, and that she and the rest of her team were going to be laid off. With those layoffs, Lesley decided that her time in an industry in which she had built her stellar career during the previous thirty-plus years was finally up. She wasn't going to try to hang on to something she felt was over just to keep up appearances. It was time to reinvent.

Lesley was confident that she was financially prepared for this kind of change due to wise saving over the years and, as she says, "paying attention to the writing on the wall" with the digital age wreaking havoc on many print publications. Still, having also been editor-in-chief of top women's magazines such as *Marie Claire, YM,* and *Redbook,* and having enjoyed the glamorous perks of being a New York City magazine editor, Lesley was rattled by the idea of losing her identity as a boss—a boss who was backed by teams, assistants, corporate budgets, and millions of readers. She was setting aside that mask. It was time for her second act. She had to reinvent herself. For her next chapter, Lesley chose to become an entrepreneur, and she says it's one of the most difficult things she has ever done. Not just because building a business can be an arduous journey, but because she had to open herself up to something she never strongly considered before: support.

Today, Lesley is the founder of CoveyClub—an online platform that she describes as "a virtual meeting place for lifelong learners." The concept for CoveyClub emerged when Lesley's loyal readers contacted her via her personal social media accounts after *More* folded, and they asked her to create something new for them. When Lesley sent out a fifty-four-question survey, 627 of those followers responded, allowing Lesley to create a road map for her new business. She realized there were women out there who still wanted the type of content she, as an editor, was so gifted at delivering.

When I ask Lesley about the transition from corporate to noncorporate life and her reinvention as an entrepreneur, she candidly responds: "It's hard." Sitting at one end of a large wooden table in her beautiful home in New York as the sunshine pours through the windows, she explains: "At corporations, the way I describe it, it is like a big rushing stream, and as an executive, you basically drop in with your little rowboat or your kayak or whatever it is, and you just start paddling away. The question is: How fast can you get in? How fast can you navigate? Where's your group? All that stuff is there for you. You just find it and you start going. When you're an entrepreneur, you have to *create* the stream. And the strangest part about it is momentum. There is no momentum if you don't create it. Nothing happens if you don't do it. It sounds like a really obvious thing, but it's not obvious to people who've been in corporate their whole lives. I mean, there were so many days in the first two years when I was putting CoveyClub together where I would sit at this table in my living room and say, 'Okay, if I go to the beach today, nothing happens, right?' It was such a weird, existential concept. If I go to the beach today, and I'm running a corporate magazine, there are thirty other people still there making it happen."

Another part of the entrepreneurial journey that Lesley says she wasn't prepared for is one that so many solopreneurs or people who run their empires from their homes, their laptops, or even their mobile phones face: isolation. This isolation is actually my why for starting the *Support is Sexy* podcast and our community of women entrepreneurs. I personally experienced that sense of isolation while trying to build a business on my own and getting stressed out because I felt like I couldn't find the answers I needed, or even just an understanding ear. I knew that there were too many of us out there who aren't just struggling trying to have it all and do it all alone. We're suffering.

"It's much more lonely than I thought it would be," Lesley confides about her own realization about entrepreneurship and the sense of isolation. "It's much more singular. I did not become a writer again, because I didn't want to be in this singular kind of business. I deliberately didn't want to do that again. And, lo and behold, I find out that being an entrepreneur is very singular and lonely as well. You're by yourself until you have funding. You can't hire a ton of people. I'm a team runner. I love having a team. But there is no team."

However, Lesley did find hope in one important aspect of entrepreneurship that she says she didn't find in corporate. "When you're in corporate life, no one says to you, 'How can I help you?'" she explains in my interview with her for my podcast.[1]

"It was such a shocker when I got out and people—everybody I met—said, 'How can I help you?'" Lesley said the concept of support was so foreign to her that she was completely incredulous. That is until she realized these supportive folks were genuine with their offers and not going to give up. "I was like, 'Yeah, right, you don't want to help me.' And then these people would come back at me and they'd say, 'Let me do this for you. Let me do that.' I'd be like, 'You want to help me, really? And you're really gonna do it?' I was completely dumbfounded. I've had at least five or six people jump in helping me with their expertise. I have someone now helping me write a pitch deck. I've had somebody come on for three months and help me get the branding right. I'm just shocked by all of these generous, kind, thoughtful people who really believe in what I'm doing. It will make you feel really good about the world out there."

When I asked Lesley why she thought accepting the support was so difficult for her, she sounded somber for a moment and admitted that the struggle to remove her mask of independence was *real*: "That was really troubling for me, Elayne. That was really hard. I was very bad at asking in the beginning and uncomfortable, really uncomfortable, at accepting. That took me about six months to a year to get comfortable with all that. And now I'm comfortable!" she said, perking up again. "You know, when your money runs out completely," she said, laughing. "I try to barter things that I can offer to people as an exchange: visibility, doing stories on them, putting them out there, connecting them with people. There are things that I realized that I have to offer that are not just monetary, but it's hard. And I find that women have a very hard time accepting help because we're the help givers. So that can be a very tough transition."

Accepting that it's time to move on, let go, reinvent, and try something new can be difficult for any woman, especially when you've fashioned your successful career and your enviable life around the certainty of your status or position for many years—whether that's as an executive within a company or elsewhere. Whether you were pushed into this new opportunity by the Universe or you made the leap holding onto nothing but faith, the transition may make you uneasy and reveal things about yourself that you never realized. And that's okay to acknowledge and accept.

But now what? Are you going to continue being isolated and alone because you're stuck in the space of the "old you" and worried about your image (i.e., your mask), or are you willing to take another courageous leap and learn how to ask for *and* accept support?

"I've seen really powerful women at some events, where you're supposed to go around the table and everybody would have an ask and everybody would have a give," Lesley shared in an example of how difficult it is for some powerful women to ask for support. "We got to this one woman who is like a major venture capitalist, written books, all this stuff. And when it was her turn to ask for something, she started to cry. She couldn't ask. It's amazing how hard it is to ask for what you need. You just have to know that that's a vulnerability and you have to be able to deal with it and learn about it, read about it, figure out how to get over it and start asking.

"The wonderful and scary thing about being an entrepreneur is that you have to finally confront a whole series of other emotional things that you didn't know might be holding you back," Lesley observes. "In corporate life, you can hide those things because it doesn't ask you to sort of dissect all of your vulnerabilities. You can find a job that plays to your good vulnerabilities and plays up your really good points. When you're on your own, you are confronted with everything."

I've often said that entrepreneurship is one of the greatest lessons in personal development. You certainly will learn what you're made of and how much grit you have, that's for sure. But you don't have to be an entrepreneur to have the epiphany that 1) perhaps you're entering a new chapter of your life (maybe it's the end of a relationship, a change in the way you're living your life, the start of a new chapter professionally, or something else) and it's time to embrace it, 2) it's okay and you'll be okay, and 3) you don't have to do it alone. I have friends who are executives at major corporations who want to transition, but understandably they feel trapped by the familiarity of the company they've been with for decades, the golden handcuffs of the big salary, the endless perks they enjoy, and the clout that comes with their position. I've told them not to beat themselves up. When the pain is real enough and it becomes unbearable, they will make a change and probably not a moment sooner. Some of us don't pull our hands away from the stove just because we sense that we're near the heat. Some of us have to feel the burn of the fire to make real change.

For Lesley, that moment of becoming more open to support during her journey of reinvention came when she just couldn't take it anymore. The fire got too hot. "When I finally realized I had to accept help, I think I just got to the point where I was worn out and I just realized I cannot do this by myself. It's too many hats. It's 24–7. You know, it took two years to pull CoveyClub together and actually get it launched, and I think I was pretty good until the launch. And then once the launch happened and it had its own momentum and I had to respond to everything and keep it going, I was working 24–7. I was working weekends, and I realized my life had become very flat because all I did was get up and work all the time. I really had no other life. It was really bad. I think that's when I finally realized, 'Look, you need help with this. You can't do this all by yourself. It's doing great, but you just can't do it all by yourself.'"

You can't. You shouldn't. And you don't have to do it all by yourself.

You have nothing to be ashamed of if you have either been released from your current position (whether that's in your professional or your personal life) or you decided to walk away and do something different. And you absolutely need to be open to asking for *and* accepting support along this journey. Don't be discouraged by the idea that you may need to learn something new or enter unknown territory. You're not too old.

You're not too stupid. That's not who you are unless that's who you believe you are. And you have nothing to prove about how "capable" you are because you've already been successful. You are brilliant, willing, and able to learn something new at any age or stage of your life, if you so decide. That's the exciting part. It may not be *easy*, but you can certainly choose to view it as exciting, so don't hide behind your mask and cling to an old identity of you as the boss who's "got this." Get support. And remember: you don't leave all of your amazing experiences, expertise, and knowledge behind just because you've left a certain position or industry. You take all of that with you, which can make your experiences moving forward in this new space that much richer.

When I first reinvented myself as a podcast host who interviews women entrepreneurs around the world, I had no idea what I was doing or where it was all going. Unlike Lesley, I didn't have the benefit of a questionnaire to help guide me in the right direction. Instead, I was driven by the kind of show that I wanted to hear, featuring the women whose stories I felt were missing on most podcasts. I didn't even know at the time that I was going to interview "women entrepreneurs around the world." That wasn't part of the plan. Truth be told, I started off interviewing my incredible girlfriends who had their own intriguing businesses, and it all evolved from there.

Even though podcasting is part of media, and I had done some work as a booker for television and radio and had been a guest on several shows, I had never been a host. I was never the person out front. An appearance here or there, even on national television like the *TODAY* show or CNN or *Nightline*, is not the same as carrying a whole show. After twenty-plus years as a writer and editor for some of the industry's top magazines and digital publishing outlets, podcasting was all new to me, and I was definitely outside my comfort zone.

As I said, I didn't know how this reinvention was going to work, but here's what I did know: I still had those twenty-plus years of experience with me. Many of those skills come in handy in the business I'm building today. In addition to hosting the *Support is Sexy* podcast, where I've now interviewed more than five hundred women entrepreneurs around the world, I am founder of SiS.Academy—an online learning platform that educates and empowers Black women entrepreneurs, who are the fastest growing segment of entrepreneurs in the United States, but often the least supported. I speak to women in organizations about the power of getting over "I got it" and embracing support as a superpower, and I am building a global community of supportive, connected women who value collaboration over competition. My previous experience creating content for audiences of women at different brands, being a storyteller who can effectively share my own journey and lessons of going from the corporate environment to entrepreneurship, those guest appearances I mentioned that now allow me to feel comfortable onstage and on camera, and my experience with brand building and galvanizing an audience all come into play. They don't fall to the side because of my reinvention. They are crucial to my reinvention, as is getting the support I need to be as successful as possible in this next chapter of my career and my life.

You can do the same. Have a willingness to learn something new, be conscious that you take your experiences with you, embrace support whenever you need it, and have a plan for your reinvention. Even though that plan will likely evolve (as plans do), have a sense of where you want to go, take that first brave step, and get some support along the way.

TAKE ACTION:
COME UP WITH A REINVENTION PLAN

Lesley, who also hosts the *Reinvent Yourself with Lesley Jane Seymour* podcast, says embracing reinvention—especially as an ambitious woman—means facing some realities. "I think you have to get to a point where you realize that your dreams can change, and that's okay," she says. As we all live longer, work longer, and have the urge to create longer, we have to realize that second acts (maybe even third acts) are inevitable.

"It's going to happen that you're going to reinvent. Either it's going to be that you're forced to reinvent because you have to move or you lose a job or you're downsized or your kid gets sick or your mate gets sick or you get sick or something's going to happen, because our lives are long and it's never going to be a straight arrow. So you have to be prepared, and you have to have what I call a *reinvention plan* in your back pocket," Lesley advises.

Whatever stage you're in—whether it's pre-reinvention or you're in the thick of it, Lesley says there are steps you can take to craft *your* reinvention plan with support.

1. Get your financial house in order. If your reinvention includes leaving your position and a steady salary behind, Lesley advises having the equivalent of a year's salary saved up that you could put toward whatever your next chapter is going to be. "You must think financially about your future, and you must have something put away to do something with," she says. "You cannot walk up to the precipice and look down into the yawning abyss with no parachute. Finances are your parachute."

2. Don't let 'em fool ya. Even if you've been with your company for decades and you feel all cozy and secure, have a reinvention plan in mind. This isn't the 1960s, and staying at the same organization for thirty years before retiring with your gold watch is rare. Even if you do retire, it's more likely than not that you're going to want to do something else after that. "People say to me, 'Oh, I've worked for this bank for twenty-three years. They love me,'" Lesley says. "But it's not about love. It's about that bank was bought a month later and everybody had to move to Alaska. Now, if you're not moving to Alaska, what are you gonna do? Of course, they love you, but what are you going to do? So, we have to be prepared."

3. Realize that side-hustling isn't just for kids. Side-hustling (building a business or additional income stream outside of your day job and regular salary) is not just a millennial move. It's a must, especially for women today as we continue to fight for parity in the workplace. Now is the time to test out business ideas and opportunities to see what you'll create beyond your job. (If you're already an entrepreneur, think: How can you diversify and expand? This doesn't have to mean you bring on a team of people. But it could mean you create additional offers for your clients and customers.) "You should have some kind of side hustle that you're doing on the weekends or at night," Lesley says. "It could be jewelry-making, it could be whatever, but with the idea of a long trajectory and thinking, could you do something with this in your future?"

4. Be a lifelong learner. "That is kind of the thing that sets the CoveyClub membership apart from everybody else is we are all lifelong learners," Lesley says. "We're always trying to improve. We're always trying to keep our brains going and keep ourselves interested and connected." Stay connected to what's new in your industry or in the industry that you want to enter as part of your reinvention. When I decided I was going to launch a podcast, I consumed every resource I could from podcasters I admired for different reasons. The internet literally has endless resources and content that you can tap into to learn about nearly anything, or at least determine your starting point (and don't forget your local library). The information is out there. Just lean into the idea of being a lifelong learner.

5. Create your "kitchen cabinet." Not quite sure what your next chapter is for your reinvention? Lesley says her "kitchen cabinet" strategy can help. "Creating your 'kitchen cabinet' is going back and pulling together an evening or two evenings with friends from when you were a kid, all the way up to different stages of your life," she explains. "Put them in a room or on a Zoom call, take a whiteboard, and start asking them things like: 'What are the words you would use to describe me?' 'What are the things that you remember that I was interested in?' You're looking for those links and those threads that were dropped along the way that we can pick up again as an adult, and you can now use them in different ways. We're taught to edit as a kid, you know. Everybody wants to be a ballerina if you're a little girl—well, 99 percent of us. At a certain point, we realize, yeah, we're probably not going to be the lead ballerina at the American Ballet Theatre. It's just not gonna happen. So, at a certain point, you've got to give that up, right? But you could go back as a financial expert. Maybe you're at the point in your life where you could find a local dance company that needs your help." When you're filling your kitchen cabinet, Lesley says, there are certain things that you're looking for in the process to see what sparks your interest. "How do you make your life have purpose? How do you make your life exciting again? How do you make your work exciting and interesting again? We've gotten rid of all those things so long ago, we can't even remember. And it's those friends who help you remember. Get them to explain who they remember you as and then pare it all down."

6. You're not done until you say you're done. As we've said, transitioning to the next chapter and letting go of a part of your former identity can be tough. But it doesn't mean that it's *over.* "It's up to you. It's not up to them," Lesley says. "That's the very frustrating part—a lot of people think it is up to 'them.' It's not. It ain't done until you say it's done."

11

Build Your Love Club

By the time I sat down for the first time in the office of business and life coach Margo Geller in 2018, I was hanging on by a thread. I had moved to Atlanta from New York the year before, and things were not going well. I was still working night and day on evolving *Support is Sexy* as a business and a brand, and trying to figure out what it could fully become in addition to a podcast. I hadn't yet found a place of my own, and—to be honest—I hadn't fully committed to staying in Atlanta, so I was living with my parents (which presents its own set of challenges for any forty-something-year-old adult). I was constantly running around with my mom to medical appointments and touring nursing homes as we tried urgently to get a family member, who was suffering with Alzheimer's disease and living alone, into a safe, full-time care facility for her own protection. I was also lonely as hell—with few local friends, no romantic relationship, and no real network in my newly adopted city. I was surviving with little-to-no money, working odd jobs to stay afloat, and desperately missing the income I used to make in New York. I wasn't even sure I could afford a coach at the time.

It wasn't long before I was in tears. It may have been the very first session; I'm sure it was at least by the second. I was ashamed of how I was feeling. But what I have come to love about working with Margo—who has a degree in psychology, a master's in social work, and is also an entrepreneur who sold her own catering business years ago and understands the highs and lows that come with entrepreneurship—is that she taught me the importance of making room for my feelings, especially anger, which I learned I have a tendency to suppress or otherwise completely ignore.

I've always seen anger as an emotion that indicates that you've lost control or that you're letting a situation get the best of you. What I've learned through working with Margo is that by not acknowledging your anger and making room for it, you're more likely to let it get the best of you, whether it clouds your judgment, causes you anxiety, or manifests physically through stress, headaches, tension, depression, or other ailments. Holding those emotions in causes lack of ease (i.e., dis-*ease*) in your body. Instead, we can choose healthy ways to release and exert that pent-up energy.

I realized I don't have to pretend to be a brick wall to build my business. I can *feel*. At the stage when I first reached out to Margo, what I was feeling was deep loneliness, confusion, and disconnection.

Fortunately, connection is Margo's area of expertise. As author of the book *The Love Club: A New Approach to Business Networking*, she has created a system to help her clients learn not only how to network, but how to build meaningful, fruitful, and supportive relationships. What stops many of us, though, as successful and ambitious women, from building these quality circles of support—as opposed to superficial relationships that don't support us or serve us when we need them—is not only our commitment to independence, as we've discussed in previous chapters, it's also our belief that since we've reached a certain level in our careers or personal journeys, we don't think that networking is something we "need" to do regularly anymore.

"It's the 'I can do it myself' [mentality]," Margo says as we catch up between our regular weekly sessions. She shares why successful women sometimes struggle to connect. "Most women who get into leadership positions or who are successful entrepreneurs really pride themselves on their independence and, as you say, 'I Got It!' Syndrome." She continues, "A lot of that is about control more than anything. It's perfectionism and it's control, and they can kinda go together."

To get over our sometimes debilitating need for independence and for control, Margo says we have to learn to build our own Love Clubs, which she describes as "a network of mutually loving relationships that bring success to all the parties." "If you want meaningful, fulfilling relationships, whether it's a client or a friend or a partner, it really helps to figure out what that person needs. Are they someone that you're going to be able to easily love? And vice versa. You don't want to work with someone when you don't feel like they like you and you don't like them."

The first step in building your own Love Club? Make a list and take inventory of who's currently in your existing contact list.

"Make a list of everybody you know or anybody who would recognize your name," Margo says. "The list could be a thousand people, especially if you're fifty-something and your whole life would go back to every tennis team, every book club, everything you've ever been involved in, and work, too."

Next, it's time to rate your relationship with each contact between 1 and 10—with 10 being the highest or most valued relationship.

Your goal is to start to build a "Love Club" of contacts who range from 7 to 10.

"Are they a potential ideal client? Are they a potential ideal referral source? Are they a potential ideal referral partner?" she asks. Margo defines a referral partner as someone who is a professional, like you are, who is in an aligned industry and who may be able to support you with referrals, such as a chiropractor being a referral partner for a massage therapist. In this example, they're in a similar field, but they offer different-yet-complementary services. A referral source, she says, is a good friend or a client who knows you, knows how great you are, and can speak passionately about what amazing work you do.

Next to each name on your list, assign the number. "If 10 is perfect—which doesn't exist—7 to 10 is kind of the sweet spot," Margo says.

After you've assigned your numbers, it's time to make some tough decisions. When coaching clients through the Love Club process, Margo instructs them to put numbers on all these relationships, and any that tally between 1 and 3, she coaches her clients on an exit plan. "We need to get those people out of your life," she says. "And maybe some 4 to 7s are then slipping into 3s, and we need to look at that and how that is interfering in creating a life that's filled with the right people."

When looking at the relationships that rate from 4 to 7, Margo says, think of them as outfits in your closet, if you need help making a decision about on which side of the rating scale they really belong. "Can you take this outfit, and—if you add a scarf to it—make it a 7?" she asks. "Once a year, I look [in my closet] and I say, 'You know, I bought this ten years ago. It felt good on me then, but it really doesn't feel good on me anymore.' I find that if I really can't see a way to get it up [to between 7 and 10], I just let it go."

Even if you're a woman who might struggle to make meaningful *new* connections, letting go of the people you're used to, who are already in your network, those you feel comfortable around (even if, deep down, you know that relationship is toxic, unhealthy, or unsupportive) can prove just as difficult. We start to accept those toxic, unfulfilling relationships as normal, or maybe we've never known anything different. Margo says that even if those people who bring negative energy into your life are family or longtime friends, you gotta let that go if the relationship doesn't nourish you and support you in the way it needs to at this point in your life. Don't feel guilty about that. Just know that you get to decide what kind of energy people bring into your space.

"You have to, again, [ask yourself]: Are these people 7 to 10s for me? Do I need to talk about my business with them or not? You have to focus on the 7 to 10s with everybody, including family and friends. Friends who say, 'What are you doing? Are you crazy?' [about your business or your ideas], you might want to stay away from them or limit your time with them."

The Love Club rating scale also comes into play as you're building your business and screening new clients or business partners, or when you're building your team with new talent. Even if it's someone you really think you want to work with or someone who has been referred to you, Margo says you still need to apply some qualifying questions to the relationship to see if it's a good fit. Some of us let way too much crap slide, ignore our intuition, and overlook red flags because we don't want to appear difficult or we're worried that another client, partner, or team member might never come along. You have to have the courage to make the choices that you know—in the long run—are best for you, even if they sting a little in the moment.

"I have had clients that I saw fifteen years ago still send me emails saying: 'Margo, you'd be so proud of me. I didn't take this client on, even though he could have paid me a lot of money.' That just makes me smile, because it's like, 'Yes, you don't need to work with people that don't feel good to you.' I don't care how much money they pay you; it's not worth it."

Depending on what kind of business or professional circumstances you're in, your questions are going to vary, but here are some that Margo asks when she's considering a new client. Use them as a guide.

- **The "Why Now" Question:** "What made you reach out for help right now? Why not a week ago? Why not two days ago? Why today? That is always my first question. I get them to really zero in on that."
- **The "Who Else Have You Dated (and Why Did You Break Up)" Question:** "One that I really, really like is: 'Have you ever worked with a coach or counselor in the past? Did you find it to be helpful?' If they say 'yes,' then I want them to tell me a little story about it. 'What was this person like? Why did you like them? Why are you not seeing them now? Why me? Why not go back to them?' This is where I pick up on personality disorders, which, because I was a psychotherapist for twenty years, I know a lot about. If somebody tells me they've just gone through a lot of counselors, and it's always about the counselor—'Well, you know, she was this and then she became that'—and they were up on a pedestal and then they became the most awful counselor in the world, I typically don't want to take on somebody who always points the finger out."
- **The Motivation Question:** "Then, another question is: 'How motivated are you? On a scale of one to ten, digging deep and being honest with yourself, are you in the 7 to 10 range? Are you really, really motivated? Because if not, maybe we need to wait.'"

What's as important as how motivated this potential new client or connection is, also consider what your motivation is. For Margo, when it comes to her work, it's not about money, it's about "love and fun."

This is what has kept her going and committed to being of service to entrepreneurs, business owners, and self-employed professionals for more than thirty years.

What is it for you? What motivates *you* to want to be in this relationship or partnership? What will you contribute? What support do you hope to get out of it? And how will you be of support for the people in your life?

You may have heard the quote from famous motivational speaker Jim Rohn, who is credited with saying, "You are the average of the five people you spend the most time with." When you're doing that math, recalibrating your support circle and writing down the ratings for your very own Love Club, remember this above all else: you deserve to have people love up on you and support you. Sometimes the obstacle is not about independence, it's not about an adverse reaction to the idea of networking or the need to be in control. Sometimes we just need to be reminded that we deserve support, that we deserve to have people root for us, cheer us on, and show us love, even if they think we're a little bit crazy or delusional for going after this dream or making whatever our next brave move is.

Your Love Club is out there waiting for you. You just have to find them and connect with them. And when they offer you that love and support, be courageous enough to accept it.

TAKE ACTION: CREATE YOUR VISION FOR YOUR IDEAL CONTACT

While making a list of existing contacts, rating them, and asking those qualifying questions are crucial to the process of building your personal and professional Love Club, you also need to attract new people into your life who are 7 to 10s. Margo suggests that you write out your vision of your ideal contact.

Here are some questions to help navigate the process. Write them out and be as descriptive as possible. As we said earlier, the Universe loves specificity. (You can also download this list as a worksheet at elaynefluker.com and write your answers there.)

- How would you describe your ideal contacts?
- What do they look like?
- How old are they?
- What do they do for a living or what kind of business do they have?
- What are their interests?
- What do the two of you share in common or how will you complement each other?
- If you're thinking about a client, what kind of budget do they have; how much do they pay you and how often?
- What pain point or need do they have that has brought them to you?
- How would you love to support this contact or be of service to them?
- What will they love about working with or spending time with you, and vice versa?

Keep in mind, your ideal contact will evolve over time, so be open to adjusting your profile as you grow and as you become clearer on what you're looking for, and what (or who) you want to leave behind.

12

Know Your Anchors from Your Engines

For as long as legendary media mogul Oprah Winfrey has been gracing our television screens, we have known about her love and adoration for her best friend, Gayle King, who is a celebrated journalist in her own right as cohost of CBS *This Morning*, a three-time Emmy Award winner, and an inductee into the Broadcasting & Cable Hall of Fame. Oprah says she and Gayle have been friends since the two were twenty-one and twenty-two and both worked at a television station in Baltimore. They've been known to speak on the phone multiple times a day during the course of their decades-long friendship.

In an interview on *The David Rubenstein Show*, Oprah shared why having a friend like Gayle in her life has been an important support system to her, and why you need the same kind of friends in your life.

"You want to have a friend who wants the most, the best, and the highest for you," Oprah said, telling host David Rubenstein that she shared this nugget of wisdom about meaningful friendships with some of the young graduates from the Oprah Winfrey Leadership Academy for Girls in South Africa who were then young adults. "I have never seen a person like Gayle." Oprah then turned to the studio audience and shared the same advice with them. She warned the crowd to beware of "friends" who act like they're happy for you when, really, there's some jealousy there, even if you sense a "teensy bit," she says. In their thirty-plus years of friendship, Oprah says she has never felt any kind of jealousy from Gayle. "Except for the one time I was onstage dancing with Tina Turner."[1]

In other words, when it comes to your friends and the people in your life, you have to be able to distinguish your anchors from your engines. And Gayle is definitely one of Oprah's engines.

This is an important distinction I was first made aware of during a *Support is Sexy* podcast interview I did with brand strategist and motivational speaker Michelle Villalobos,[2] creator of the Superstar Business Breakthrough Program. Michelle, who shares how it took her nearly seven years of trial and error and struggle to make money in her business before she had her own breakthrough by way of a mentor and business coach, spoke about the importance of knowing the difference between those two very important groups of people in your life: your anchors and your engines. This is especially important if you're doing something that may be considered risky, that's outside of your comfort zone, that's taking you to your next level, or that differs from everyone else's expectations of you.

Michelle defines anchors as those who hold you in the same place and, as a result, hold you back for their own reasons—whether they are conscious that they are doing this or not. It is in the same way an anchor is used to hold a ship in place. Michelle makes clear that if someone is an anchor, this doesn't necessarily mean he or she is a "bad" person. "It doesn't mean that the person doesn't love you or even that they don't believe in you," she explains. "But generally an anchor is someone who is concerned more with your safety and security than with your full expression or with you stepping into your full potential."

I caught up with Michelle on a video call to dive deeper into this topic more than two years after our original podcast interview when she first mentioned this concept to me and totally shifted my point of view on people who frustrated me because I felt like they just didn't get it or understand me. Now I know better, and I'm able to manage those relationships better. Michelle shared more of her own personal experiences with managing the anchors in her life and gives tips on how to maneuver your relationships with your anchors, particularly when they're close to home, which can make it even more difficult to understand and accept.

"I grew up in a very traditional home, very strict, and I learned at a very young age that I needed to please my parents," Michelle says of her Cuban upbringing. "That was my strategy for 'survival.' So, from a young age, I looked to my parents for approval on everything. I'd bring my report card home and say, 'Look, Mom and Dad, I got straight A's.' Their appreciation for that was my world, and I didn't realize that I carried that pattern well into my adulthood, especially when I became an entrepreneur. I would come running to my parents and say, 'Look at this idea I have.' And they'd be like, 'You're gonna rent a place for $20,000 and make a big, huge women's success summit? Are you sure that's a good idea?' And then I'd think, 'Oh, maybe that's not a good idea.' So, anchors can be people who are the voice of reason, logic, and rationality. But if I had run my life and my business by logic and rationality, I would not be where I am right now," says Michelle, who has since hosted several sold-out events around the United States.

How do we, then, cut those anchors loose so we can move on when they are people who love us and want us to be safe? Michelle says, we don't! "We don't need to cut them loose. That's my favorite part of this. We just need to reorganize whom we communicate what to."

In the case of her parents, Michelle says she stopped sharing ideas with them and started sharing results. "It changed our whole relationship, the whole dynamic," she says. "Soon, my mother was carrying my business cards around in her purse and bragging about me because I was so 'successful.' Nothing really changed, except that I stopped telling her about the things that are on my mind and that weren't yet complete, versus the things that I had already signed, sealed, and delivered."

On the other side of this equation, there are people who are your engines. "An engine sees the biggest and best version of you," Michelle says. "An engine sees your potential. And they see you as on your way to your best self. So, whereas an anchor might see you as the version of you who was seven years old and badgered them for a flute until you got one and then played one lesson and then quit ["I use that story a lot," she laughs], the engine sees you as the version of you who is disciplined and who is committed once you find the thing that you're meant to do. The engine helps you see that future version of you. The engine witnesses you when you do things that are aligned with the future version of you."

I have had to cut loose a few anchors in my own life and reframe my relationship with others, especially since becoming an entrepreneur and leaving what appeared to be my "good job" working as a journalist in New York, making a six-figure annual salary. Instead, I traded that life for the uncertainty of building something out of nothing with an online business, where I get to do what I love by coaching women around the world, fostering a global community for them to connect, and creating best-in-class content and resources for them to learn, grow, and thrive. Most people don't see that vision, however. They just see that I don't have the same kind of seeming stability. (Although *stability* is a difficult word to use when applied to any job these days. Even if you have a steady nine-to-five, get your side-hustle on, boo.)

These relationships were particularly challenging for me in the early days of my business when even I wasn't sure that it was all going to work. (And some days, to be honest, I'm still not. Outcomes are never guaranteed, but my hard work and dedication to my vision are.) I can understand why some people don't have the stomach for that type of uncertainty. It isn't easy, that's for sure. But, for me, this is just part of the journey on my way to my vision. What your anchors—or those who doubt your success based on where they believe you are in your life right now—don't realize is that your current circumstances do not dictate your future success. Your habits and your hard work and your commitment to that vision do. Circumstances change. And if you are reading this book and you are an ambitious woman who is as dedicated, determined, and hopeful about your success as I believe you are, your circumstances can sometimes change pretty quickly if you are diligently working to develop habits that serve your best self, and you are doing everything within your power to shift the narrative of your ever-evolving story, to turn things around in your business or career, or to take your life in another direction. Don't let your anchors try to convince you that this is as far as you're going to go. They don't have that power. When I encounter people like that, I think to myself, *Thank God they* ain't *God.* Faith will carry you further than fear every single time.

I'm fortunate because, in spite of the anchors, I still have plenty of people who are engines in my life, and I thank God for that every single day. I don't know what I would do without them. But I admit, even though I'm wise enough to know better, it can still be tough to know there are people whom I love very much who will never support me in the way that I wish they would. Again, it's not because they're bad people; it's just their mindset, their point of view when it comes to work and success—what that should look like and what that means—and, in some cases, it's simply a generational divide. Work, for example, looked very different during the period in history when you would stay at one job for thirty years and only venture into entrepreneurship if you were crazy (maybe that hasn't changed so much), if you were considered completely unemployable, or if you had access to capital or your family's investment to support you as you built your business. It's a chasm that I have tried to close for years until I finally realized that these anchors were bringing me down, figuratively and literally. I decided I cannot accept any threat to my dreams that might take me under. I don't accept those fears and limiting beliefs as my own truth. So, as Michelle said, I reconfigured my relationships in my own way.

Reconfiguring those relationships for me means simply not sharing my every move with them, just as Michelle advises. It's better if they don't know, because frankly, they just can't handle it. And it's better for all parties and for our relationship if I don't give them the opportunity to project their fears and doubts onto me.

Instead, I depend on my engines for that support. They have the capacity to hold my vision, whereas my anchors can't handle the weight.

Your engines may be friends and family, but if that's not an option for you right now, look to coaches, mentors, teachers, therapists, counselors, and other advisors in your life for this support. I even consider some people I admire, who have no idea who the heck I am, as my engines. Women like Oprah Winfrey and Lisa Nichols and Michelle Obama and Sara Blakely and Marianne Williamson and Dr. Brené Brown—women who motivate me from afar through their work, their open-heartedness, their generosity, and how they courageously show up in the world. Your engines don't have to be your besties; they just have to be the best people for you to look to for inspiration and support at this stage of your life.

Those people—the ones who, as Oprah says, want "the most, the best, and the highest for you"—will prove to be your most powerful assets of all.

TAKE ACTION: RELEASE YOUR ANCHORS AND REV UP YOUR ENGINES

When you're taking inventory of your anchors and engines, Michelle suggests this simple exercise (which she adapted from one of her personal engines, Ben Shemper of Abundant.is): Make a list of between one and twenty people in your life who have influenced you in some way. Next to each person, Michelle says simply write an "A" for anchor and an "E" for engine. This isn't a list that's meant for you to share with anybody else. This is for your own clarity and assessment of the relationships in your life, so be honest.

Michelle says, consider: "Is this person driving you forward toward your full self-expression, toward your full glory? Or is it someone who's trying to keep you safe in the same place, or who actively holds you back and criticizes you?"

This list, if you are honest, should help make this crystal clear. "You're going to either recognize that you have a whole bunch of anchors, and you need to reorganize those relationships, or you have a whole bunch of engines, and you need to reach out and say, 'Thank you and I appreciate you.'"

13

Seek Wise Counsel

I laugh when I think about it now. There I was, happily bouncing from seminar to seminar at the July 2018 Podcast Movement conference in Philadelphia, surrounded by my peoples—a sort of nerdy, eccentric hodgepodge of individuals who were connected by their love of the art of audio. In just three days, I was scheduled to head off for a trip of a lifetime—traveling to several countries over the next several months and living within each country for a month at a time—with the travel company Remote Year. During the trip, which had already been in the works for nearly a year for me by that point, I planned to interview women entrepreneurs in each country I visited for the *Support is Sexy* podcast and share their journeys with my audience.

As host of *Support is Sexy*, I had already interviewed hundreds of women entrepreneurs from all parts of the world from my home office (i.e., my bedroom), using tools like Zoom (thank you, internet), but I believed that conducting in-person interviews with a woman entrepreneur from Marrakech, Morocco, while in Marrakech, Morocco, or a woman from Valencia, Spain, while in Valencia, Spain, or a woman from Sofia, Bulgaria, while in Sofia, Bulgaria, would take my podcast to the next level. I was thrilled about the possibilities.

At about lunchtime between sessions at the conference, I headed to the lobby of the Philadelphia Marriott for a call with one of my biggest clients at the time, a technology start-up based in Atlanta with which I had been working since January of that year, and I thought would be a client until at least the end of the year. In fact, I was *depending* on them being a client, as the $10,000-a-month consulting fee would help fund my trip, which cost $2,000 per month for travel, accommodations, a work space in each city, and local events.

In addition to the trip, this client fee also allowed me to finally secure much-needed support for my business through contractors, whom I planned to keep onboard while traveling, including writers to create content, podcast editors to help me continue to release new episodes of *Support is Sexy* five days a week as I was very proud of doing, a podcast booker who helped me find and secure amazing guests for the show, and a digital marketing agency that supported me with social media for the *Support is Sexy* brand.

Um, did those plans work out? Turns out, not so much.

My call with the start-up's new head of human resources was cordial but brief. The client was ending my contract as of July 31. The date of our call was July 24. I was scheduled to leave for Valencia, Spain, that Saturday, July 28.

My heart sank into my stomach. For a few minutes following the end of our call, I sat there and just stared at the wall. The bustling lobby seemed to move in slow motion. *I will not panic, I will not cry. I will not panic, I will not cry,* I repeated in my mind until I could see (and think) straight. How was I going to do this? As I mentioned, this company was my biggest client at the time. It was the only client that had been steady for the last six months. And, yes, though we were on a month-to month contract, I naively assumed that any changes would be given to me with at least a thirty-day notice. Not seven days.

(Note to self and to you: Always, *always*, have a clause in your contracts that requires at least a forty-five-day notice of any change and explicitly states that you will be paid for that last month of the contract. Protect yourself from awkward moments that can blindside you.) But hindsight is an evil cow, and I didn't have time to fool with that heifer in the moment. All I could think was: *What? Am? I? Going? To? Do?*

I made my way through the lobby, painstakingly smiling at fellow podcasters along the way, until I reached outside in front of the hotel. If I were a smoker, now would have been the time to blaze up a cigarette or two. (Cigarettes are bad for you, kids. But you understand the pressure.) Some of the questions that went through my mind:

1. Should I go into the bathroom and weep or scream or both? (And it should be said, yes, I was mad at the company for cutting me off so abruptly, but I was more upset with myself for not preparing for this possibility.)
2. Should I head back to my girlfriend Erica's house, where I was staying while in Philly, and pack up all of my stuff that I had brought along for my trip and just head back to Atlanta?
3. Should I say "screw it," not tell anyone that this had happened, and just go on the trip and figure it out along the way?

Fortunately, I decided not to explore any of those options. Instead, I sent a text message to Margo Geller, who had actually connected me with this opportunity for the contract with the technology company in the first place and who, at that point, had been coaching me for about seven months. I decided not to have a meltdown. I decided not to give up on my dream because of this setback. I decided not to close my eyes tightly and avoid it and just hope it would go away.

I decided to get support. And having a coach I could trust saved me from spiraling into negative self-talk and taking any immediate, and likely irrational, action.

Margo talked me down off the ledge of fear, where I was dangling by my well-manicured fingernails by the time we chatted on the phone. I paced back and forth outside the hotel and nervously blurted out what happened, and she created the space for me to talk through my feelings, as she always does. Fear, anger, confusion about my next, right move—all of those emotions were swirling around inside. Being able to get those emotions out—and knowing that she was there to support me through it without judgment—was invaluable.

One of the tenets of Margo's practice as a counselor is: "First, feel. Second, solve." Too often, she says, we want to skip over the emotions and jump to the solutions, which could cause us to make decisions through clouded judgment fueled by anger, disappointment, or sadness—or, on the other end—high emotions like excitement or elation, which can also cloud our judgment.

So, after first creating space for my feelings, Margo and I began to solve and walk through some of the practical solutions. I needed to cancel any unnecessary contractors that I currently had for the business right away to eliminate those expenses (and give them *proper* notice). What other clients or potential clients could I focus on while I was traveling? What other income or revenue did I have on the horizon? What credit cards could I responsibly utilize to hold me over, if needed?

One thing we agreed on was that I would not, absolutely not, turn around and head back to Atlanta. I needed this trip. For myself. For my business. For my podcast. And, for this very book that you're reading now. I had received my book deal just two weeks before leaving for the trip, which is something I told my agent, Nick, was part of my vision. Getting the book deal and writing a book for a major publisher like HarperCollins Leadership was a dream come true. Getting a book deal and writing a book while traveling the world and working and living in a different country each month was like *insert exploding brain here.* And I believed that this trip could only make my book that much richer by way of my experiences and my personal transformation through this journey.

I also decided during that call with Margo that I wasn't going to share this situation with anyone else but her that day. As I mentioned, I was staying with one of my best girlfriends, Erica, while in Philly that week for the conference. Another dear friend of ours, Atiya, along with Erica's sister, Tia, were driving up that evening from Washington, DC, so we could all spend some quality time together before my big adventure.

Now, these chicks are my sisters. I'd known them all for more than twenty-five years by this point, and I can talk to them about anything. You hear me? Anything! Still, I decided that this wasn't the time to share. Not because of shame or fear of judgment from them. They love me, and I know that. But I didn't want to put that weight on them, and I didn't want them to project the weight of any fears they had onto me. Fears that, of course, would have been out of concern for me, but fears nonetheless that I just couldn't carry at the time. I had plenty of my own, and if they had sensed any of that, I would have put them in a situation where, even by way of supporting me, they would have been anchors to me.

Turns out that was the right decision for that night for many reasons. We all gathered in Erica's beautiful home, popped a couple bottles of wine, ate way too much pasta, danced around clumsily for hours to Ciara and Beyoncé, and laughed our asses off until the tears flowed down our cheeks as they helped me unpack all my crap, and then harshly told me what I was not allowed to bring with me on the trip. (I admit, I had packed too much stuff. After much negotiating, I eliminated one whole bag and was then proudly down to only three! All the other stuff filled a large plastic bin that I would leave at Erica's house until . . . whenever.)

What I didn't do was wallow in my fear and bring my sisters into that dark space with me. Instead, they were unknowingly every bit of light, love, and support that I needed that evening to relax and stay in the moment.

And Margo, with her advice as my coach, was every bit of what I needed to stop me from making a rash decision out of fear. Her insight was crucial. Had I not had my relationship with a coach that day to be a sounding board, offer sage advice, and give honest feedback at that critical moment when things fell apart, who knows what my choice would have been?

Having a go-to source to support you during those times of uncertainty who—sometimes—may not be one of your besties or your life partner is vital to your well-being and to your success. A coach, a counselor, a mentor, a therapist—you need an objective and trusted source in your corner. Someone who likely has seen crisis time and time again with other clients, who has practical ideas about what steps to take to help you make the best decision for you, and who probably has a different context than your friends do when it comes to your triggers, your fears, and your goals. Individuals who provide feedback with the intention of edification rather than humiliation.

A coach was an absolute must for SoulCycle cofounders Elizabeth Cutler and Julie Rice. When the serial entrepreneurs partnered up in 2005 to create a cycling studio they felt was like no other—one that had a certain kind of vibe, created a sense of community, and inspired riders in ways the founders felt other gyms and studios at the time failed to do—they had no idea exactly where their relationship or their business idea would take them. They also had no idea how quickly the SoulCycle concept and its passionate following would catch on, making it a challenge to keep up with the fast-paced growth of the business.

When their third cofounder decided to leave the business after just three years, Elizabeth and Julie not only had to deal with the logistics of this change, but also the emotions. How did they handle all the challenges? They decided to reach out for support. They got a coach.

Elizabeth was the first to jump in—drawn to find a coach at the time because of the difficulty she was having juggling her booming new business and her family obligations. "I had two small kids, and I had a business that was on fire and that was such a mission-driven business," Elizabeth tells me via phone after finishing a hike near her Colorado home. "I just felt the deepest, most compelling energy to get this thing out to the world because I knew what it was doing for me and I just wanted to share that with people." Although her husband, who had his own demanding career, helped out with accounting for the business occasionally, Elizabeth says she was doing much of the work herself, along with her cofounders. When the business partnership started to come undone beneath the pressure of SoulCycle's success, Elizabeth said she felt like she hit a wall. "I remember thinking, *'Oh my God, I now have business issues and relationship issues,'*" she says. "I was hitting the wall on the personal front and hitting the wall on the business front. And I didn't have the time that I needed to be able to take care of myself or do the things that I needed to do for my family and take care of my little kids." So at 11:55 p.m. one Sunday evening, she googled "NYC life coach," and the decision forever changed her life.

"Meredith changed my life in the first meeting," Elizabeth says about her coach. "We sat down and she helped me look at my schedule and bucket things so that I could find space in my life. It was like finding more days in the week. It was so powerful. I went to Julie and I was like, 'Listen, I had this really powerful session with this person and I feel better and I really needed that. Do you want to talk to her together?'"

Julie agreed, and Elizabeth says their time working together with a coach helped make SoulCycle—and their partnership—a phenomenal success. They learned how to communicate better, understand each other's point of view, and get to know each other's world as they made decisions about how to move forward in the business. Opening up to a coach, Elizabeth says, helped the pair evolve as leaders. "There's nothing that can evolve on its own. That's not how it works."

Today, SoulCycle has grown to include more than eighty studios around the United States and Canada and has a cult-like following (yours truly included!). In 2016, the pair sold SoulCycle for $90 million, *each*! More than a decade after starting their first business together, Elizabeth and Julie continue to be business partners, continue to work with a coach, and decided to start a new venture, LifeShop, which will support other entrepreneurs using many of the tools they learned during their entrepreneurial journey.

"Look, I would not be married to my husband without these tools, and I would not be married to Julie without these tools. I mean, I might be, but it wouldn't be as good a marriage, you know?" Elizabeth laughs. "For me and Julie, having a coach is awesome. We tell everybody to get a coach, like, at the beginning. Why wait?"

When you're looking for support, especially when the ground shakes beneath you and you may feel thrown off in the moment, make sure you seek wise counsel that can offer a level head and steady hand in the midst of it all. That stability and insight might be just the support you need not only to make it through a tough time, but to go to the next level.

TAKE ACTION:
WHEN IN THE MIDST OF
WHAT FEELS LIKE A CRISIS, PAUSE

1. Sit still, plant both feet on the ground, and take a few calming, deep breaths. In for four, hold for four, out for six, hold for two. In for four, hold for four, out for six, hold for two. In for four, hold for four, out for six, hold for two. Feel your chest expand. Feel your head get a little lighter. Envision yourself inhaling light, power, and positive energy. Exhale and release any anxiety, tension, or limiting beliefs. Close your eyes during this exercise, if it's safe to do so. (And by *safe*, I mean if you're not driving a car or flying a plane, not safe like no one is watching. If other people are around, who cares? Screw that! This is about you getting grounded and re-centered.) Ever since learning about this popular breathing technique from my friend and former *Essence* magazine colleague Robin D. Stone, who is now a licensed mental health counselor, I use it often to calm my nerves and relax—especially before making decisions under pressure.

2. Do not take immediate action. Give yourself some time to let your emotions settle before you make any decisions. A few hours, if you have them. Overnight is even better, as long as you don't spend the night steaming in anger or self-pity or buying a huge purchase like a car or house just because you're excited about a new contract. Your goal should be to let it ride for a little bit and put some space between your emotions and the occurrence that has temporarily rocked your world—whether you consider that occurrence "good" or "bad." Remember what Margo advises: First, feel. Second, solve.

3. Don't throw it all away. Sometimes we don't even make a decision. We don't take time to breathe. Instead, we just toss our hands in the air, give up, and throw the whole thing away without considering what some of the other options are. Don't do anything hasty that you might regret once you have some time to breathe, step back, and gain some perspective.

4. With a clear mind, reach out for support from the person who is going to respond to you with a level head. I could have called my mom when things went left and I lost my client, but she literally may have had a heart attack. Even though I'm in my forties, she and my dad are constantly worried about their entrepreneurial daughter, who is always doing something they'd consider risky. They had enough fears about this months-long, multi-country trip already.

I could have hopped into the middle of a kiki session in a group chat with my squad of girls and told them what happened. Yes, they would have supported me, I'm sure; but it may have turned into us circling about the issue of why the company I had the contract with would do this as opposed to solutions for what I could do about it.

Instead, I chose to reach out for the support that felt like what was wanted and needed at that time. I called my coach, an experienced, licensed, professional counselor, who has seen drama far deeper than mine—which gives her perspective—and who knows my story, my secrets, my triggers, my insecurities, and perhaps most important, my dreams. Margo was clear about just how much this trip meant to me, and she knew that my only goal in that moment was to figure out how to make this work.

When the ground shakes beneath your feet, reach out for feedback and support that can bring you back to center and help you make wise, balanced decisions from a place of power rather than a place of fear, revenge, or self-sabotage.

By the way, I am currently writing this chapter of my book while sitting on my terrace in Valencia, Spain, while traveling with Remote Year. This was definitely the right decision.

14

View Feedback as a Gift

Some of us are accustomed to viewing feedback in just one way: criticism. But if you shift your perspective on feedback, be open to it, and view it, instead, as information that you have the opportunity to process, analyze, and apply as you see fit in order to support you, it could be exactly the fuel you need to lift off to a higher level, personally and professionally.

For Lisa Sun, founder of Gravitas clothing line, feedback from a former boss ultimately changed the trajectory of her life nearly a decade ago. A then-twenty-something, Lisa was working at a global consulting firm at the time, and when she went to her boss to find out how she was doing, she received a less-than-glowing review. Though Lisa's performance, at that early stage in her career, wasn't the issue, there was one important thing that her manager felt Lisa was sorely missing: gravitas. Lisa's boss advised her to own her power, and to buy new clothes that better represented that power.

During our interview for her appearance on the *Support is Sexy* podcast, Lisa relived that pivotal moment in her life and explained her boss's rationale. "When I asked her why, she said: 'Well, Dumbo had a flying feather. He didn't actually need the feather to fly. He could always fly. But he needed something to hold on to, to confirm a self-belief.' And she said, 'For me as a woman, when I wake up in the morning, I put on something that makes me look good. I give myself a compliment in the mirror. You need to find something. It doesn't have to be clothing, but you need to find something that every morning gives you self-belief and helps you see something positive in yourself. Seeing yourself very positively is actually the most important thing for other people to see. If you can't pay yourself a compliment, no one else will.'"[1]

Instead of shrinking or taking offense, Lisa said she embraced this challenge from her boss and chose to view the feedback through a different lens than most might. "I took that feedback as a positive," she said. "I took that as this person really wants me to succeed and that's why they care enough to tell me."

Lisa stayed with that company for eleven years, until she decided to step away for a year of family time, travel, self-reflection, and space to decide what she wanted to do next. It all came full circle when, inspired by that same conversation with her former boss, Lisa decided to launch her Gravitas clothing line in hopes of inspiring other women to embrace their power. "We started in clothing mostly because the woman who gave me the feedback told me to buy a new dress," she explained. Lisa said she also liked the idea of using clothing as a superpower because she saw the dressing room as an analogy for our lives.

"When you are a little kid and your mom says, 'Let's go shopping for a new dress,' you are really self-confident. You're born self-confident, and you're so excited. After your teenage years, [with] body image and a whole bunch of things, the dressing room almost becomes a place of anxiety where you bring self-loathing, you bring all your insecurities, you just set yourself up to fail. We [at Gravitas] bring joy back to the dressing room, because I always say, 'Stop fitting into something. Find something that fits you.' Clothing gives us a very powerful way, quite immediately, to experience what I think all of us should practice daily, which is feeling something good about ourselves," she said, sharing that she hopes her clothing makes women again feel the joy of that carefree six-year-old who's happy to be out shopping with Mom. "We like to say that our mission is to catalyze confidence."

Soliciting and embracing feedback for Gravitas is something Lisa continuously used in the development of the line early on. "Four months into the journey, we had a set of samples and a name and some branding," she shared on the podcast about those early days. "And in February of 2013—seven months before we turned on the website and started to sell our products—I had two hundred people in my home, so five people every night for forty nights. I would just invite friends, colleagues, and mentors, and I would let them beat up on my business. I'm not one of those entrepreneurs who says, 'I'm working on something I can't tell you about it.' I actually think we all walk around with a million ideas. I think everyone has good ideas. It's [about how] you execute it. So I don't think of anything as confidential or you need to sign an NDA. I'm very much about, you put it out in the world because people will beat it up."

One example of how courageously requesting this kind of feedback paid off for Lisa in her business was when one of the women who attended her beat-up-on-my-business session said, "Oh, I think Oprah is gonna love this." Lisa said that person sent one email that led to a game-changing moment for Gravitas. "The next day, the creative director of *O, The Oprah Magazine*, Adam Glassman, was in my apartment giving me feedback," Lisa shared, still sounding surprised. "Then they featured us in the November 2013 issue [of *O* magazine]. Gave us two pages, which changed our lives. We'd been open six weeks, and he changed our lives."

And that former boss who gave Lisa that feedback about buying a new dress to help boost her confidence as a young career woman? She ended up being one of Gravitas's angel investors.

Lisa's experience with receiving feedback when she was in her twenties also influences the way that she now gives feedback to her own employees or the young women in her life. "One thing I love is that quote from Indra Nooyi, the former chairman and CEO of PepsiCo, where she says: 'The mentor chooses you. You don't choose the mentor. So make yourself very measurable.' I've used that as a philosophy to a lot of the people I work with, which is that feedback is a gift. And what I've taught people is, you can't go and just say, 'Could I have some feedback?' Because when you say to someone, 'Could you give me some feedback?' they always say, 'Oh, yeah, you're doing fine. Just keep doing what you're doing.' It's like the natural reaction because we really don't want to make time for it. And so one of the things I did early on in my career—and what a lot of people who work with me now do—is [ask]: 'Is there one thing I could do better?' I was actually pretty well known for having this little section of my notebook where I would catalog the 'one things,' and as soon as I mastered them, I would cross them off. So I tell people, when you ask for feedback, just say: 'Is there one thing I could do better?' Because everyone can come up with one thing. And [then] when you ask them, 'Okay, how do I do that?' they will be very open to helping you work through that one thing."

Consider: How do you digest feedback from trusted sources in your own life? Do you leave the conversation focused on your bruised ego, or do you make a decision that you're going to think about what was shared and see how you can do better? If you're open to it, the right feedback can support you and take you far.

TAKE ACTION:
CURATE YOUR CIRCLES OF INFLUENCE

Lisa said what she has learned throughout her journey as an entrepreneur about creating these powerful feedback loops that have helped her grow her business is that you have to curate your circles of influence. Think of these circles as concentric, with you at the center, and with different groups of advisors occupying each.

1 .Your Inner Circle: The first circle, Lisa advises, is your inner circle. "Those ten girlfriends you sometimes don't want to hear what they have to say; but they're the ones who are actually going to be tough on you. There's always the inner circle that you really want to hear what they have to say because when things are tough on the entrepreneurial journey, those are the ten men and women on whom you rely to tell you: 'Hey, I've seen you since day one. I've seen you working out of your apartment, and I know you can do it.' So I always say that that first concentric circle, the inner circle, you have to invite in [and say]: 'I want you to be part of my success. I want you to have your fingerprints on this.'"

2. Your Mentor Circle: Lisa explains that the next concentric circle is composed of your mentors. "I'm an older entrepreneur, right?" she asks rhetorically during our interview. "I'm someone who worked eleven years in corporate America before deciding to do this. So I had a really nice group of people, whether they were former bosses or former clients, whom I invited in to see this. And that was because I really wanted more seasoned expertise looking at the business."

The mentors who occupy this circle should be seasoned and experienced within their field of expertise. So, even if they are not in the same industry as you are, you should feel confident that you can trust that their feedback is coming from a space of knowledge.

When I first met one of my mentors, Richard Nailling, through the nonprofit organization SCORE, I went into his office with the intention of asking about marketing advice for the media and content consulting arm of my business—advice he definitely gave me. But what neither of us knew at the time, Richard's background and success as a television executive would prove extremely important as I eventually decided to focus on growing the *Support is Sexy* platform and began to have conversations with television networks. Now, after each of those conversations, appointments, or ideas, one of the first things I do is send a note to Richard to update him and get his feedback. In return, he mentors me with his advice through the lens of his many years of experience in television, as well as his insight as a successful entrepreneur. That advice in large part helped me secure *The Elayne Fluker Show*, my upcoming television show that celebrates women of color entrepreneurs in Atlanta.

Without having Richard as a part of my mentor circle, I would be making my best guess (and probably plenty of mistakes) as I pursued this chapter of my journey. Why waste time with your best guess when you can find a seasoned mentor who can support you with the best advice they have based on their experience?

3. Your Distant Friends Circle: The outer concentric circle of people to support you is what Lisa calls your "distant friends circle." This circle is composed of folks she considers "friends, but not frequent friends." "I had someone I mentored at McKinsey," Lisa shares as an example. "He was a business analyst. I'm friends with his parents on Facebook because his father was my doctor. He helped me in an emergency situation where I had this terrible flu and [my mentee and I] were traveling and he's like, 'My dad's a doctor. You can go see him today.' I became friends with them on Facebook and his mother, God bless her, lived next door to the person who was, at the time, the executive editor of *People* magazine. And this lovely woman, Karen, said, 'You know, I'd love to come see what you're working on and maybe I'll bring my next-door neighbor with me.' So, there is that outer circle that you never know when you put something good into the universe, who's going to want to help. Everybody wants to help someone. People get a kick out of it! So when you give permission to people to just be joyously helpful, it's such a lovely thing when you're creating a business."

Lisa says, as you're curating your circles, continue to take those tiny steps to build your business at the same time. You're not sitting around and waiting for support and feedback before you even get started or before you take that next step; you're being open to it and inviting it along with you for the journey.

"If you're starting a business, take the tiny steps, do the little things. Buy the domain name, set up an email account, go register your LLC, or get a trademark. All the little things that make you feel like you're really doing it. And then, three to four months in, even if you have a day job, even if you work on other things, just host people in your apartment and have coffee or treats and let them see what you're working on. It doesn't have to be formal. It could be a couple prototypes and your logo and what you think they're going to stand for. Everyone will have ideas to bring to the table." Lisa says even if you don't take all of the ideas—which you should not feel pressured to do—you can benefit in many ways from this strategy.

"There is also accountability," she says, "because being an entrepreneur—especially if you're going to self-fund the start of it—it's not like you have a boss to answer to. [This way], every time you see one of the people who knows what you're working on, they'll say, 'How's that going?' One of the things that really helped us [when hosting] a couple of those sessions I did was my former employer said, 'Well, why don't you come when you're ready and do some preorder trunk shows at the office?' We took probably five hundred preorders even before we started making product, just from people trying on the samples [at that trunk show]."

You never know.

SECTION THREE

Let Go of the "How"

"The how happens as you take each step."

—Michelle Khouri,
founder of FRQNCY,
on *Support is Sexy* podcast

15

Show Up for Yourself

We can talk all day about how to get comfortable with support, ask empowering questions, take off that mask, be open to feedback, and stop being Superwoman for everyone else. But now it's time to consider one of the most provocative questions that I think you'll ask yourself when it comes to support: *How are you showing up for yourself?*

Be honest: When you say you're going to do something for yourself, do you follow through or do you flake? When you promise you're going to be somewhere—like, say, an important doctor's appointment or a yoga class or a course you've been wanting to take, do you get there on time or do you show up late? When you say you're going to finally cross that lingering dream off your to-do list, do you get it poppin', or do you continue to procrastinate?

As the saying goes: how you do anything is how you do everything. And if you do anything that illustrates your lack of support for yourself, your wellness, and your own dreams, the Universe—and the people around you—will follow suit. This isn't about beating yourself up; but it is about being real with yourself and understanding it might be time for a personal check-in on what's really holding you back. Sometimes the reason we have such a difficult time requesting and accepting support from others is because we don't know what it looks like or feels like—not just from someone else, but from ourselves. Remember: you're looking for support, not a *savior*. So, the best support really starts with you showing up for you.

In this way, support is much like love. You want the experience of it, you want people to know how to give that experience to you, but is it an experience you have not yet fully given to yourself? Is it a gift you've had access to but never unwrapped? And if that's true for you, how can you have that expectation of others? How will you know what that support—that love—looks like and feels like if you don't first give it to yourself?

I bet you do everything you can to support everyone else, right? So, what's up with you doing it just for you? Think about it: When was the last time you did something supportive just for you? Not *by* you. *For* you.

If the answer is never—or maybe you can't recall the last time—hit the reset button and consider today Day One. Decide that from this day forward, you will be much more conscious, much more loving, much more committed, much more intentional, much more gracious, and much more supportive to yourself. Dare to put yourself first, which includes making sure you know that you deserve support, and surround yourself with people who you know have your back and who are your engines.

Another important part of putting yourself first is creating space for your dreams. I know you're an ambitious and accomplished woman.

And perhaps, to everyone else, you appear as though you've already ticked every single item off your dream list. But I'm referring to those dreams and goals that maybe you never tell anyone about, the ones that keep coming to you, and no matter how much you bob and weave and ignore them and push them down and stay busy doing everything else, they won't go away. The ones that you may have set aside for years so that you can take care of everybody else, or do what you think you're supposed to do rather than what you're meant to do. That dream that just keeps calling you and calling you (like Pookie in *New Jack City*), and then it calls back because you have yet to answer. Yes, *those* dreams. Even if you're at the top of your game, it's likely you still have other dreams that you want to fulfill. So, what are you waiting for? Stop stalling. Now is the time.

For me, getting a book deal was that dream—one I had longed to fulfill from whatever moment I first learned that this was how books got out into the world, through a publisher. Of course, times have changed and so have the avenues of publishing a book and sharing your ideas, but my dream never waned. I wanted a book deal. And thanks to my agent, Nick Chiles—and several revisions of my proposal during the course of a year—I received one.

When I submitted the first draft of this book to my editor at HarperCollins Leadership, I was terrified. But it was time! I knew I did my best with writing it while I traveled and lived in five different countries during my trip with Remote Year, and I felt good that I had delivered the manuscript (close to) on time. But I also knew that I was coming up short—literally. If you asked me to guess, I would have told you I had written at least eighty thousand words while I was traveling. *Seriously.* But in actuality, I had written about thirty-five thousand words—way short of my goal of at least sixty thousand, per my contract. As you can imagine, when I saw that "35,000" pop up in the Word Count field just a few days before my due date, I freaked a bit . . . Okay, let me keep it real: I freaked *a lot*! I basically had written half a book. What was I going to do?

I emailed my editors immediately. I figured that was better than trying to push out thirty-five thousand more words in two days, right? I was honest about my gross miscalculation and asked if I should hold off on sending the first draft in. "Send it anyway," they told me. So I did. Now, not only was I nervous about getting the manuscript back with the proverbial red pen markups writers always talk about from their editors, but I also cringed at the idea of not delivering enough—which taps into a major insecurity I have overall. Whether it's with my work, in my relationships, or anywhere else, I never want to be thought of as not enough. What I have to remind myself is that, no matter what anyone thinks, I already am enough.

So, when the response came back from the HarperCollins team, I didn't get the red pen markup, but the news I did receive was an arrow through the heart. My editor gave me good feedback on my "voice" as a writer. They liked the tone and thought I was on the right track as far as the direction I was taking the book. However, the manuscript was too short, which we all knew. What I didn't know—and what they communicated to me as gingerly as possible—was that because I'd have to go back and write more, *much* more, the publisher was going to push my book release date back. (Later, after speaking to Nick, I learned that this frequently happens with book projects, for different reasons. Dates change, and publishers move projects around. But at the time, I sunk into a puddle of I-am-not-enoughness.)

I was told to take my time, work on a second draft, and keep them posted. So that's what I started doing, working on my second draft. Or at least that's what I told people I was doing whenever they asked, "How's the book going?" I'd respond with some version of "I'm working on it." The truth? I stopped showing up. I was paralyzed with fear that my next version—and any version after that—was not going to be enough.

Can you believe that this B.S. of me pretending I was writing went on for six whole months? Yep, *six*! Sure, I took notes here and there and scribbled ideas for additional content I could add to the book when a bit of inspiration struck me. But I wasn't *writing*, writing. And there were even a few sympathetic friends who volunteered to read the first draft and give me notes and feedback.

One of those sympathetic saints who volunteered to review my draft was Shavonne Holton, who is a longtime listener of my podcast from the very early days, and with whom I've now had multiple chats over the years via email and Zoom. Shavonne owns an independent book publishing company, VK Press, which she started after she began listening to *Support is Sexy*. She provided me with copious notes on my draft. I'm talking thoroughly annotated notes. I appreciated it so much; but, yeah, it still wasn't enough to get me to show up at my laptop and get to typing. I was stuck because I couldn't figure out "the how." How was I going to write thirty thousand more words and keep it interesting?

Then Shavonne happened to come to Atlanta during her cross-country move to California. She reached out to get together while here, and we caught up for an early lunch at a restaurant in downtown Decatur, Georgia.

Having given me such great feedback on my book, Shavonne asked about it and how it was going with my rewrite. I fibbed and said some version of, "I'm working on it," even though I was still stalled. Sometime later, our conversation turned to social media, another albatross around my neck when it came to things that I knew I needed to do, but hadn't. I confided to Shavonne that, because I wasn't traveling or doing anything I felt was visually stimulating or particularly exciting, I had pretty much stopped sharing and engaging on social media with thousands of connections—which, if you didn't know, is a *huge* social-media no-no. "People don't want to see me just working," I said and shrugged.

"Yes, they do," she quickly responded. "People love to see other people working on different projects. It makes them feel like they're a part of the process."

Our conversation continued, and we eventually said our goodbyes. But her words to me lingered. She believed people would enjoy seeing me working. *Really?* Here I was thinking that I wasn't doing enough (there's that word again: *enough*); yet people like her, and possibly a few others, might be interested in seeing what I was up to. The journey, not just the glossy result.

Inspired by the conversation, and though nervous as hell about how to do it or what was even the point, I decided that I would "go live" on social media (for the very first time, I should mention) and talk about writing this second draft of my book. My intention was to be honest and authentic, and to share what "that thing"—that dream—was for me that I had been putting off. In addition, because you know I'm all about support, I planned to encourage others who might tune in to the live chat to work on their thing, too.

Day One of this experiment of mine was Monday, June 24, at 6:30 a.m. EST. I began first by showing up on Instagram Live every morning, and a couple days later, on June 26, I posted on my Instagram page @supportissexy and "officially" invited my followers to join me each morning. And guess what? Several of them did! A few days later, on June 30, I began showing up simultaneously on Facebook Live, since I had a private mastermind Facebook group with hundreds of women there. Even while on vacation during a long Fourth of July weekend in Savannah, I showed up. Even when I was exhausted at 6:30 a.m. every single morning, I showed up. Even when technology didn't fully cooperate with me (which happened often), when I didn't exactly know what to say, I never knew what to expect, and I knew that it was far, *way* far, from perfect, I showed up.

I. Showed. Up.

And you know what happened? Other women began to show up, too! And during that half hour, they worked on *their* thing—from books to screenplays to their websites and more that they, too, had been putting off. There were things that they were afraid to even begin because of fear of failure or rejection, or because they had convinced themselves that it was a silly pipe dream. There were things that they, too, didn't think would measure up and be "enough." But they showed up. They showed up because I finally let go of the "how" and showed up. And together, while supporting one another virtually, we showed up for each other and worked for thirty minutes each morning on that thing.

As time went on, I began to notice some of the same women joining me at 6:30 a.m. every single morning over the first few weeks. And, thanks to some wise counsel, I decided to make the group more formal and show up to offer support to women who committed to being part of a private group coaching program that I created, called the Support is Sexy Inner Circle—women who were willing to pay to be part of this collective. This meant they got a daily coaching call with me at 6:30 a.m. each morning as a part of the package, along with exclusive online masterclasses where they engage with and ask questions of top women entrepreneurs, gain access to a private library of content that's just for them, and receive consistent support for "that thing" that they've been longing to make a reality. Four incredible women signed up and invested. And within just the first few weeks of spending time with these women as part of the new Support is Sexy Inner Circle, they each shared how much the group had brought out of them—professionally, as related to their dreams for their businesses, and, more powerfully, personally, as far as how they're making moves in their own lives with much more confidence. By showing up and leading by example, I gave them a reason to show up as well. On top of that, they helped hold me accountable for writing the second draft of my book by reminding me how much it's needed in the world. And if you're reading this now, then I think it's safe to say, mission accomplished.

It's time for you to show up, sis. Let go of the "how," stop stalling and stop waiting until it's "perfect," because while you sit there stuck in neutral, your big, hairy, scary, audacious dream or goal is out there waiting for you. But it won't wait for long. Eventually, it may move on to someone else. And won't that be a shame?

Have you ever had a dream or idea that you've been harboring for years and then, suddenly it seems, someone else comes out with the exact same idea? You wonder how they could have known what you were thinking and you secretly swear that they must have used some kind of witchcraft to steal that idea straight out of your head.

But they didn't. It wasn't witchcraft; they did the work.

I believe what award-winning author Elizabeth Gilbert wrote in her book *Big Magic: Creative Living beyond Fear* when it comes to ideas. Ideas are everywhere and they want to manifest in this world, whether that's with you and through your brilliance, or with someone else. You may have a lot of reasons (excuses) for why an idea passed you by. But if you're honest with yourself, it is likely you were either too distracted to notice the opportunities available for you to take that leap, or you were playing small and you resisted the voice that may have said, "Now is the time." Again, don't beat yourself up. Just do a personal check-in. What's the truth? Face it, and know that you can make a different choice starting today.

Don't let that burning desire that you're aching to bring to life move onto someone else if that's not what you want. And don't get stuck because you can't immediately determine how you're going to bring it to life. There are plenty of paths to your destination or your destiny. You're not restricted to following one road just because everyone says that's the way you're supposed to go. You don't have to commit to doing it a certain way just because that's the way so and so did it. And, just because you've been successfully doing one particular thing or had a career in a field that's different than the one your current aspirations fall into doesn't mean you have to stick with that first career forever as people might have you think. As we discussed in Chapter 10: you have the power and the right to reinvent.

Look at Ava DuVernay. Today, Ava—entrepreneur, writer, producer, director, and film distributor—is one of the most celebrated creatives in Hollywood and a groundbreaking director who, among many other accolades, created the hit television show *Queen Sugar* for the Oprah Winfrey Network. She is the first Black woman to helm a film that grossed more than $100 million with the film *A Wrinkle in Time* and she created culture-shifting projects such as *When They See Us*. But before she broke through in filmmaking, Ava was a publicist with her own successful Los Angeles–based boutique public relations firm, the DuVernay Agency. Over the years, the DuVernay Agency worked on campaigns for projects by well-known directors such as Steven Spielberg, Clint Eastwood, and Michael Mann. I'm sure some may have thought Ava would be crazy to give up her celebrated business and her career, which she had built for more than twenty years when she decided to pursue her dream of directing in her thirties. In fact, Ava told CNN's Van Jones on his television show, "I didn't pick up a camera until I was thirty-two years old. I didn't go to film school. I was a Black woman trying to make film at that late age. And in film, that's old. That's like dog years."[1]

Ava DuVernay, the director, now makes powerful documentaries, narrative projects, and commercials, and she has her own film distribution company and collective—ARRAY—that is "dedicated to the amplification of independent films by women and people of color globally," according to the company's website (arraynow.com). She is also the first Black woman director to be nominated for a Golden Globe for the film *Selma*, the first Black woman to win the Sundance Film Festival's

U.S. Directing award with her beautiful film *Middle of Nowhere,* and the first Black woman director to be nominated for an Oscar for her powerful documentary about the criminal justice system, *13th.* And she's just getting started.

Your journey is your journey, and your dream is your dream. Don't allow yourself to be held back by your age, your current skills, your current resources, or your current circumstances. The key is to, as tennis legend Arthur Ashe says in one of my favorite quotes: "Start where you are, use what you have, do what you can." (I actually have this quote framed on my bookshelf as a constant reminder to myself whenever I get stalled and overcome with fear when pursuing my own big and scary dreams. And trust me, it happens often.)

But remember: you're not in this alone. Part of showing up for yourself is letting the Universe know that you realize you need support along the way, and that you have faith that support is available for you in abundance. That's why our "Take Action" exercise in this chapter is all about you being clear about what kind of support you believe you could use from other people to help facilitate this dream. No more theories around why you should ask. It's time to do some asking. So, get ready to create your very own *"Support is Sexy* List!"

Now, listen: Will the support always come in the exact way you outline on your list? No. Will it always be in the perfect package or from the person or company or organization you were certain would be there to support you? I guarantee that's a no—not all the time. But there is power in writing down your goals, in getting started, and in reaching out to people to let them know what you're up to. Not only does it help hold you accountable to the actions that you've committed to taking toward your dream, but studies—such as the one conducted by Dr. Gail Matthews at the Dominican University of California—show that writing your goals down and sharing them make you twice as likely to be successful in achieving those goals.[2] Dr. Matthews, who evaluated

267 participants from around the world of various ages and industries, found that only 35 percent of those participants who kept their goals to themselves and didn't write them down were successful, while more than 70 percent of those who wrote down their goals and shared regular updates with a friend were successful. There's power in writing it down and power in support. Just ask the women in the Support is Sexy Inner Circle.

Again, you don't have to have everything figured out before you make that first move. (No one really has *everything* figured out anyway.) And you don't have to know exactly how you're going to make that dream a reality. In fact, trying to figure it all out before you make that first move will likely cause you to be overwhelmed and end up with analysis paralysis—which will result in you spending more time analyzing what you think your next move should be than actually making your next move. It's about progress over perfection. So, just write it all down, declare that you will show up for yourself each day, and be dedicated to consistently taking one imperfectly perfect step after the other until you're closer to that dream.

I hope you're as excited about this step you're about to take as I am. Because this isn't something you have to do for yourself; this is something you *get* to do for yourself. There's a huge difference, so be intentional. You will mess up. You will stumble. You may have moments when you're scared. But you get to decide the most important aspect of this journey: whether or not you keep going or you give up on your burning desire or dream, and whether or not you struggle alone or you get support. You get to take action today that will move you forward in a meaningful way.

As I've said, in every relationship, you teach people how to treat you by the way you behave in relation to yourself. So make sure you're clear that you love and support yourself, that you only want the best for yourself and you're clear that you deserve it. Write it down, claim it, then show up for yourself by taking inspired action while also being open to the opportunities, people, and possibilities waiting to flow your way. This energy will emanate out to others in your presence and attract those to you who can help you manifest your dream, because it'll be *so* irresistible on you.

TAKE ACTION: CREATE YOUR *SUPPORT IS SEXY* LIST

In bold letters at the top of a sheet of paper or in your journal, write "*Support is Sexy* List." (Yes, really!) This is a list that's just for you, but you need to feel really good about it and know that the people and organizations on this list are there because they're going to be an important part of your incredible journey to your dream.

On this list, write at least ten resources, organizations, tools, and people (a mixture of all is even better) that may help you reach your goal. Don't overthink it—just write. Don't worry if you actually have contacts for them—just write. Don't waste time considering all the reasons it'll never work—just write. There are no right or wrong answers here—so, just write!

After you have at least ten possibilities written down, give yourself a concrete deadline (I'm thinking tomorrow) to begin reaching out to these resources. If you don't have a phone number or an email address for them, don't fret—Google is your friend, boo. Start there.

As you reach out to each, take note of their responses and record how and when you're going to follow up. I do this in a simple Google Docs spreadsheet for the contacts I reach out to every single day—whether that's a potential new client or contact or someone I'm just reconnecting with to see how I might support them in some way, or a company or organization I've heard about that might be able to support my projects via a partnership. I have a column with notes of our interaction so I can reference it when I follow up or have an idea I want to share that may help them. To me, this spreadsheet signifies that I am serious about this outreach, that it matters to me. It's not casual or haphazard. There's intention there.

Be diligent and be consistent in your outreach. Even if they say no, you're on the move now. You've put that dream in motion and you've put the Universe on notice by showing that, "Hey, I'm going for this, for real! Don't you give my idea away!"

This is a tactic that I use whenever I've identified a big dream or a goal that scares me to death, but that I know I can reach by taking one small step at a time, by looking at what I can make use of in the moment to jump-start the journey, and by being deliberate about reaching out for—and being open to—support.

Each day, and with each step, you get a little bit closer. Remember: little by little, a little becomes a lot. After you've made your way through your list of those first ten resources, start a brand-new one, begin again, and keep showing up.

16

Let People Show Up for You

Relationships can sometimes be the most difficult place for us to ask for the support we need and to let the people we love show up for us. Sometimes it's because we don't want to disappoint those people or have them think less of us (even though we know they love us); other times it may be that we don't want to burden them with having to worry about us. Or maybe we simply don't know *how* to make that ask in that moment, so instead we don't ask at all. It's complicated, right? Unfortunately, denying our needs doesn't mean we simply move on like it's all good. This can cause us to hide our true emotions and feelings from those we love or to lash out about unrelated matters when, really, we just need their help. What we have to remember is that the people who love us most are often the people who wish to show up for us most—that is, if we'd just let them.

Six years ago, Katherine met Nikki at a conference for entrepreneurs and the two became fast friends—best friends, actually. Nikki, a photographer who lived in Canada, had married at age nineteen and given birth to four children with her husband. Katherine, a life coach living in Portland, Oregon, had separated from her husband and was a single mom raising her daughter at the time. The friends bonded over motherhood, which was important to them both, and other shared interests such as business and art. Over the years—and unexpectedly to them both—they realized that they wanted to become more than friends, and their platonic relationship blossomed into a romantic relationship. The couple dated long distance for a year and a half, and five years ago, after Nikki divorced, they decided to make it official and get married. Katherine packed up her life in Portland and moved to Canada to start a new life together with their blended family of five children and a dog. It was no small adjustment.

Then, in 2016, Nikki came to Katherine and told her that *he* (which is how he will now be referred to) had come to terms with something he'd been secretly wrestling with since childhood. Though assigned female at birth and given the name Nikki, Nick had always known that he was, deep down, a boy. It was time for him to come out and live his truth as a transgender man. (Note: I used Nick's old birth name of Nikki here with his permission, to clarify the story. In general, it's a faux pas to use a transgender person's "deadname," and I want to acknowledge that.)

Upon hearing Nick's news, Katherine was supportive, but stunned. She admitted she needed a minute to process it. What would this mean for their marriage and for their family? How would she adjust to the physical changes in her partner? How would they explain this to their five children? The couple didn't have all the answers; but they knew what was going to be crucial for them both during this transition: support.

When I catch up with Nick and Katherine North, they are at their home in Canada and preparing for a family vacation to the Bahamas the following day. After considering my question about how important a role support played for them during that time in their lives, Nick says the support came in many variations. He let go of what it looked like, communicated what he felt he needed, and allowed Katherine to show up for him. "Her support showed up in a lot of different ways," he says, sitting close to Katherine during our video call. "It looked like being there to let me vent when I needed to. It looked like being there to help me find solutions that I couldn't see because of the panic that I was in at the moment. You know, when you're in that fight or flight mode and you just can't possibly see a way out of something and then someone else will say, 'Oh, there's a door, try the handle.' She was really good at doing that for me. She was great at letting me know that I was lovable and worthy when I didn't think that I was, which I think is a universal experience for transgender individuals. I think that lots of us think, 'Oh, because I'm trans, I feel unlovable.'"

He continues, "She was that touchstone for me to go back to that let me know that I was okay and that I was worthy. And when I couldn't see for myself, she could see for me, and when I couldn't hope for myself, she could hope for me. And then there were times where she just had to like shut up," he says, laughing. "There were times when what I needed was for her to just not say anything and let me have a fit. And some-times I needed her to be the angry dragon for me, who was holding the boundaries, who was protecting me. I needed her in a lot of different ways. And the hard part was being able to figure out what version of her I needed at the time and articulate what support looked like."

Katherine and Nick both say they got to this place of knowing how to show up for each other during Nick's transition and throughout their marriage by way of "a lot of therapy," which is yet another way of letting someone show up for you when you need it most. If you're struggling with communication in your relationship—especially if you've gotten to the point that you're not communicating at all—consider getting support from a therapist or family counselor. Counselors can support you with breaking down those walls that prevent communication (if that's really what you want), and they can help you fight fair and hopefully find a resolution. "We have a therapist who was able to sit with us while we had our fights," says Nick about what helped him and Katherine learn to communicate their needs clearly, honestly, effectively, and with love.

"I think Nick's transition was so intense that it forced us to learn how to ask for what we needed," Katherine says. "Which is harder than it seems to say, 'What I need from you is for you to hold my hand or sit with me quietly while I cry.' There was so much that we had to work through and figure out, and I think it pushed us to get good at that kind of uncomfortable asking."

Uncomfortable asking. There are plenty of reasons many of us steer clear of support in various situations—whether in our own families, from counselors, or otherwise—without realizing it. And sometimes, as Katherine says, it's the discomfort and the vulnerability of admitting that we need it and then being in a position where we have to ask for it that is the real barrier for us. As we've talked about throughout this book, as an unapologetically ambitious woman, you are used to having to have all the answers, or at least feeling like you should. I think it's important for you to recognize that this isn't only true when it comes to being a boss or keeping up appearances in order to elevate your career or your business. "I Got It!" Syndrome can also negatively impact your personal relationships, especially if you suppress your need for support. This goes beyond simply not asking for help from someone else; this involves not even acknowledging it to yourself, which can create dysfunction in your relationship and negative emotions within you.

"It's very vulnerable in some ways to say what you actually want, you know?" says Katherine. "Whether that's help around the house or it's a certain kind of intimacy or, in my case, it's almost always alone time. But just to tell him that feels kind of vulnerable."

Katherine, who has guided more than three thousand women to clear clutter from their lives as their coach through her company, Declare Dominion, says that this vulnerability, and the way we perceive it, causes many of us as strong, powerful women to think that making an ask and letting people show up for us exposes us. "I think it can be a way of exposing what we often think of as our weakness, and sometimes that feels really scary," she says. "It's easier to keep up—'I got this, everything's fine.' It's actually a very, very tender thing to show someone else what you need and what you actually want. Then the asking becomes like a very intimate kind of communication. It can open up space for more tenderness that you might not have even known you wanted or were craving."

TAKE ACTION: TRY A LITTLE TENDERNESS

In the exercise for this chapter, Katherine shares tips for how to confront that uncomfortable asking and open yourself up to a little tenderness.

1. **Own it.** "I think first you have to own what you want," Katherine says. "I think this is why we feel so scared. Maybe we don't fully allow ourselves to claim what it is that we really want; then even the slightest hint of judgment feels so terrible and awful—it's kind of devastating. There's almost like a preliminary step where you have to say, 'You know what, this is what I want, or this is what I need,' and you have to own it and just learn to stand in that. 'This is what I need, this is what I want, this is the help that I'm looking for, this is the favor or the support that I'm looking for.' Say it to yourself and acknowledge it and own it without

shame or blame. It's incredibly powerful. And once you do that, then other people's reactions matter so much less."

2. Make the ask. It may sound simple, but Katherine says you have to push yourself to make the ask. You won't want to; all the negative self-chatter will get in the way. But as motivational speaker and author Mel Robbins says in her book *The 5-Second Rule: Transform Your Life, Work, and Confidence with Everyday Courage*, you have to launch into action before you allow that fearful part of yourself to take the lead and take over your thoughts. This can happen (or be prevented) in a matter of just five seconds.[1] Commit to asking, and then make the ask.

3. Be specific. The Universe loves specificity, and so do the people from whom you'd like to get support. Katherine says it's important that you are specific when it comes to your ask. Not sure exactly what you need? Don't let that be an excuse. I tell the women I coach that even if you're not sure exactly what you need to request as part of your ask in the moment, you can communicate in detail what you've done so far, what you're attempting to accomplish or experience, and what you feel the roadblock is that you're currently encountering. This way, at least the person has some idea of where he or she may jump in to help—whether that's now or later. Write this out so you can see it on paper and have it in your mind when it's time to make your ask.

4. Be willing to negotiate. "This is where working with our therapist has just been super helpful," Katherine says about the need to learn how to negotiate with your partner. "It's a matter of identifying, 'All right, I may not be able to give you 100 percent of what you want from me, but I can give you 80 percent.' One of the themes that's helpful for us is to come up with some bare minimums. So, when we were long distance, we agreed that we would talk on the phone for at least an hour every night.

And that was something that we did, no matter what kind of crazy day we had. I think we had loopholes for book club night. It wasn't like you didn't get to have a life in any way, shape, or form."

For Nick, the phone calls were a must. Since they weren't in the same city, they had to negotiate a way to connect. "To know that this is when you're going to call, I can count on you to show up when you say . . . That was really important," he says.

5. Have some nonnegotiables. While negotiating with your partner is important, Katherine and Nick both say the nonnegotiables are just as important. For them, it's date nights and quarterly retreats. "We take a quarterly retreat, just the two of us," they share. "Sometimes it's a trip that's off [somewhere]; sometimes it'll just be, you know, a night in a hotel downtown. But we commit to taking time away from the kids and work and everything else." Over time, the couple confesses, they've had to negotiate on this nonnegotiable a little bit. But they realize that doing so broke down a routine they worked hard to build. "It's really caused us, I think, relationship issues," Katherine says. "So I feel a renewed sense of, like, 'Oh, this is really important. There's a reason that we made this commitment, and it's important that we stick to it.' Those are things that we agree on in advance and then we can each count on them."

6. Know that you deserve support, and remember your why. For Nick, a brand strategist and also a coach, the reason he believes many women don't ask for support is because, deep down, we don't think we deserve it. How do you combat that? He says remember your "why," because more than likely, you are driven by a "why" that is outside of yourself. Nick believes that for most women, our why is about the ways we can support those around us. So why would you deny those you serve of the best you have to offer just because you were afraid or felt unworthy to ask for support? "If you're having a hard time asking for support, or if you're having a hard time asking for the thing you need, I would say that there's usually an issue where you don't believe you deserve it and you're having a hard time claiming that you deserve it. Can you believe in your heart that you deserve that thing? Are you able to say it out loud? And if you can't . . . my thing is, *why* do you want that thing?

"I've never met a woman who wanted this thing, and it's completely selfish, and it has no good value in the world at all," he continues. "That's not how women function. Yes, they might want to gain material wealth, but that's because they want to give it back in this other way. They want to provide for their kids. They want to provide for their mother, and they want to provide for their families. There is always some good and noble reason when you get right down deep to the core of what you want.

"Remember your why and then you'll get to the deserving it part," he continues. "But when you can't get there first, this is a hack you can use when you can't have your own braveness. It's like when I go get up onstage, and I have to give a speech and I'm terrified. I remember that, 'Oh, I am doing them a service. I get to be able to do it for them instead.'"

17

Embrace a Little Grace

This is a moment that I imagine any mom would want to be there for her child, smiling proudly and taking Facebook-worthy pictures that she can't wait to post as she watches her nine-year-old daughter be recognized at her school's honor awards ceremony. This is a can't-miss moment. An unforgettable moment parents share with their children. A moment that makes a parent joyous and full of pride and helps define what kind of parent one wants to be. A moment no parent would miss.

But Dr. Traci Palmer Baxley did just that. She missed the moment. The devoted-yet-busy mom of five was working late at her job at a local university where she is a professor who teaches and works with graduate students on their dissertation research. Her daughter's big day totally slipped her mind. That is, until the crushing moment when she saw photos of her teary-eyed daughter with her best friend and her friend's mom—a mom who *was* there and who sent the pictures to Traci via text message.

"I cried, I cried, I cried. I believe my heart stopped beating when those pictures popped into my messages," Traci says when I ask her what she did when she realized she had missed the important event even though she had every intention of attending and being there to celebrate her daughter. Traci says those pictures were especially painful because she could see that, although her daughter was smiling and putting on a brave face, she was very sad and upset. "I cried, I cried, I cried," Traci says again. "It was the first time that I really felt like I had let her down. I went to her and I cried and I said: 'I am so sorry. I just totally got caught up with work and forgot. And that's on me. But I'm sorry.'"

Traci said her daughter was forgiving, told her it was okay, and said that she understood. Instead of celebrating with the school that day, the two of them went out and did something special by themselves. "She was resilient, as most kids are," Traci says. "But that was really gut-wrenching. I think that may be the moment that I gave up the idea of balance because it wasn't working."

At the time of our interview, Traci's daughter was nineteen, so this pivotal moment for Traci occurred ten years earlier, and she still remembers it like it was yesterday. You can see on her face that some of the guilt lingers, even if just a little bit.

Traci isn't alone. Many working mommies, or those multitasking with life, work, family, kids, and some of everything else, speak about experiencing what's been labeled as "mommy guilt." It's a conversation I hear often among my closest mommy friends and my coaching clients who are moms, and who are doing their very best to show up in every way they feel they need to in all areas of their lives. Mommy guilt is commonly described as the regret moms experience when they feel they have failed their children's (or society's) expectations or they don't get everything right. And many may feel even guiltier if they can't do it all and do it all right and do it all right now, and do it all right now without any support.

Since I am not a mother, I turned to psychotherapist and mother Robin Stone for insight on the psychology behind "mommy guilt." Robin believes this stems from anxiety, doubt, and self criticism that crop up and lead moms to question their fitness to take care of their children. "A lot of us allow ourselves to be bullied by cultural and societal expectations," the licensed mental health counselor in Midtown Manhattan says between videoconferencing appointments. "And it can start pre-partum. 'Are you going to eat that? What kind of birth are you going to have? Are you going to have a doula? You're not going to have a doula?!' You may start to think that you can do no right as a mother, and that can be very distressing."

Robin says this feeling is compounded for many moms by the tendency to compare themselves to the perfectly curated images they see of motherhood on social media. "That's a part of the societal expectations and our own expectations from seeing the Instagram stories and the Facebook posts and forgetting that what people share on social media is a curated life. It's the thirty-fourth take out of eighty photos or the video that they did twenty-two times to get just right. And there's this sense that our lives have to be that way."

Every mom's experience is unique, of course. But for Traci, she realized she had been trying to live up to the example set by her own mother. "I grew up with a mom who, I felt like, did everything and did everything right," she says. "It seemed like she did it without support. And so, when I first became a mom, I felt like I didn't want to be a disappointment and had high expectations because of the role model that my mom was. I kept thinking that if she could do it all, why can't I, you know? And so I didn't ask for a lot of help and I felt a lot of stress."

The only problem with that theory is that even Traci's mom tells her she's doing too much. Or, at the very least, she is definitely doing more than her mom ever had. "My mom would say to me: 'You're doing way more than I used to do. I didn't do all the stuff that you do. You have more kids than I did, and you're doing more activities and juggling more.' But when you're raised by that kind of independent, powerful Black woman, you feel like that's what you need to do. And that way of thinking was more detrimental to my parenting than anything else. I had to let go of that mindset," she says.

With this mindset shift, Traci said she finally had to get over "I Got It!" Syndrome as a mom. She began to turn to her sister circle of friends, even if it was just sharing her own struggles with them and discussing one another's insights and tips based on what was working for each of them as parents. "People are happy to help," she says. "So, I have just decided that I can't do it by myself, nor should I have to, especially when I have such a great support system around me."

That close proximity to support for Traci, as she eventually realized, wasn't just within her circle of girlfriends who were happy to help; it also includes her children, whom she had to enlist to help her as well. She says she and her sisters grew up doing chores around the house because it was a nonnegotiable. But she didn't instill this policy with her older kids right away. She let their busy schedules of school, sports, piano lessons, and so forth add to the mommy guilt of asking them to do too much. Instead, she tried to do everything herself and focused on keeping the kids involved in all the activities outside of the house.

Plus, with her children taking advanced classes in school, Traci thought chores should be the last thing on their minds. "I let those outside things get in the way of having the nonnegotiable activities, like chores, inside our home," she says. Though her kids might pick up after themselves once in a while, for the most part, Traci had taken responsibility for keeping everything clean and organized. "I think by picking up after everyone, it made it harder for me to keep up with everything," she reflects. "And so I finally had to say, 'You know what? I can't do this by myself.'"

It took a moment for everyone to adjust, even Traci, who admits she still has to stop herself from redoing all of the chores and learn to relinquish the precise folding of her towels to one of her youngest children. "They weren't done right! I wanted to go and refold them," she admits. "But you know what? He's doing it now. I'm letting it go. However they get in the closet, they get in the closet. I've had my husband take them out of the dryer and just shove them in the towel closet. I'm like, you know what? I can pretend I don't see it, be grateful they are out of the dryer, and close the bathroom closet. I let go of having my house in perfect order. There's always something that needs to be picked up around the house, so when company comes, I need to know you're coming. Don't just drop by," she says, laughing. "You will have to stay outside until we're ready for you. I even struggled to hire someone to come over once a week to help me clean because I wanted to make sure I really cleaned before the housekeeper could come over to clean. It sounds ridiculous saying it out loud, but I know many moms can relate to that. I'm okay with that now. I'm okay with that."

Traci says she had to become okay with letting go and embrace a bit of grace. Not only did she release the guilt of needing and finally accepting support, she had to decide to release what that support looked like. As an in-demand coach helping moms avoid fear-based parenting, she also reframed what receiving that support, especially from her children, says about her as a mother. She realized that having their help not only allows her to keep the chores in order around the house (even if they're not completed perfectly), but it aligns with her powerful practice of social justice parenting—a philosophy she created that is rooted in radical love and activism, and helps parents raise independent, compassionate, and socially conscious children. By not struggling to appear as a do-it-all-perfectly mom and allowing her kids to show up for her, Traci says she's allowing her kids to show up for *themselves* as well. "I was over-parenting," she says candidly. "You know, I wanted my kids to have all these things, but I was really denying them the opportunity to grow up, to be more independent. I mean, we always had a lot of conversations in my house. I questioned my kids a lot, I pushed them academically and all; but I did take away a lot of their growth by doing for them all the time."

Letting go and showing yourself a bit of grace is something that Robin helps her clients who are mothers learn how to do as well. She makes it clear that she's not in any way encouraging mothers to neglect their children. She does, however, share the concept of "the good enough mother"—a phrase coined in 1953 by British pediatrician and psychoanalyst Donald Winnicott. You're never going to strive to do less than the best for your child, but Robin says the "good enough mother" principle lets you know that "you don't have to get everything right. You can make mistakes and, in fact, mistakes can be healthy for your child to learn to tolerate disappointment and that mommy isn't perfect. It can be reassuring for a child to hear a parent say, 'I made a mistake, and I'm sorry. I didn't mean it, or I didn't mean it that way. I didn't mean to hurt you.' It's important for your child to recognize that you're human, that you mess up, too, and still know that their world is going to be okay."

If you're a mommy and you can relate to the mom guilt of not being able to do it all and do it all alone without support, ask yourself: *Does it really have to look a certain way for it to be okay for you to accept the support you need? Does it really mean that you're incompetent or unfit because you couldn't juggle a thousand balls in the air with ease?* (By the way, *no one* can.) *Does it really indicate anything negative about you at all?*

Yes, there may be fear of outside judgment, but we can often be our own worst critics, saying mean and degrading things to ourselves that we couldn't even imagine saying to other people. As a result, we put these barriers up to protect our image and our ego, whether we're conscious of this or not. But once you let go of what that support looks like, you, like Traci, will realize that support may show up in the most surprising ways. And, just as Traci discovered, giving yourself some grace and letting that support in—especially from those who love you and whom you love—can do as much for them and their development as better human beings as it can do for you.

TAKE ACTION:
LET IT GO

1. Get over perfection. In her TEDx talk on social justice parenting, Traci spoke about the importance of showing your children the moments you mess up, or when you're sad and angry, because, as she says, "They need to know all of those feelings are real and that none of them are bad."[1] Instead of hiding, Traci says you have the opportunity to model for them what they can do in a positive way by acknowledging those emotions and addressing them. "What we do with [those emotions] and how we demonstrate how to work through them is really important," she says.

2. Forget about balance. Traci says she cringes at the idea of "work-life balance." "I think, as women, we're always trying to find that balance, and I just don't think it exists. [Instead], I look at it as this idea of trying to live in harmony with all the parts of your life. There are going to be some weeks that my job has more of me than my kids, or there are some weeks that I'm like, 'I can't do that job because my kid is in crisis mode.' Or, I have not looked at my husband in a week and I need a date night. So it's not about balancing because there's never a balance. It's about really embracing the ebbs and flows of the different aspects of who you are and rocking with that."

When it comes to work-life balance, Traci suggests you throw the whole damn thing away. Decide that you're going to give what needs attention the attention that it needs, when it needs it, with no guilt, and then be able to pull it back to something else when the time is right. Pursuit of that "balance," she says, is "where a lot of our stress comes from. Instead, go with life and give the attention where it needs to go, when it needs to go there."

3. Show yourself some grace. Are you going to get it all right all the time? No. No one does. But in those moments where you mess up, show yourself a little bit of grace. As an unapologetically ambitious woman, I have no doubt that you're doing your best. That's all you know how to do! When things don't go exactly as planned, don't allow yourself to dip into shame and guilt. Show yourself a little bit of grace.

Although Traci was extremely upset about missing her daughter's award ceremony, and she expressed how upset and apologetic she was to her daughter, who was loving and forgiving, Traci also had to forgive *herself.* "I think it's also an opportunity to show our kids how we forgive ourselves," she says. "It's another way of teaching our kids to be gentle and kind to themselves. And to be simply human."

4. Be authentic. Part of the stress and the guilt of not being perfect comes from the need we have to portray a certain narrative to those around us. Traci says you can free yourself from that by being real, *really* real. "It's not going to all look good every day," she says. "It's going to be very hard some days. But give yourself a break and be okay with that."

Traci believes being authentic not only frees us, but it is a way of freeing other women as well through our stories. "As women, we need to be more open about our lives not being perfect so that we don't feel like we're walking this journey by ourselves," she says. "You can support people just by saying, 'It's not working for me,' or, 'It's very hard.' Or like, for me right now, I'm having issues with one of my kids making some decisions that I don't necessarily agree with. I need to be talking about that as a woman, who is a parenting coach. My life is not perfect either. I have to try things a million different ways and a million different times to try to make things work. And so I think by being authentic and saying that I struggled, too, really makes us better at what we do. Then another woman is supported in that."

SECTION FOUR

Believe in the Possibilities

"Everything that I want to create is available to me, when I understand that I am a possibility."

—Sylvia High,
Transformation Coach
and CEO of Aiming High,
on *Support is Sexy* Podcast[1]

18

Adopt a Possibility Mindset

hope, at this stage of the book, you realize that support can come in many different forms and within many different segments of your life—from your career to your business to your friendships to your romantic relationships. Even in the ways you practice self-love. I hope you also understand that how you accept (or refuse) this support affects all aspects of your life.

Be honest with me here: Do you really believe in the possibilities that are available to you when you open up to support? No, *really*. Are you as open-minded as you can be about how, where, when, or through whom support may come to you? Do you believe that the Universe is there to support you and help you cocreate the life you envision? Do you understand that you do not have to do this alone? And that you are not meant to do this alone? Or is there some part of you that is still incredulous and holding onto the limitations of your current circumstances and all the reasons that you believe support won't show up for you this way? You're approaching this whole support thing like, *Sure, it might work for everyone else; but not me,* right?

I totally understand that, if this is a concept you're not used to hearing or that you haven't thought about in this way before, you may have a bit of apprehension about the possibilities that support can provide you. But listen: nearly nothing conjures up as much hope as believing in the possibilities, especially when things seem highly improbable or even impossible. And nearly nothing will give you access to the support that you deserve as being open to the possibilities because, honestly, they're endless! This is how we learn to experiment, come up with new concepts, try new things, exercise our imaginations, see what works and what doesn't, and get better acquainted with what we love and what we don't. When we believe that more of what we want to achieve or contribute is possible, we can take ourselves even further, even higher.

This isn't just the woo-woo part of me talking to you. (Although, if there's one thing I love, it's the woo-woo.) Psychiatrist Dr. Srinivasan S. Pillay, a world-renowned keynote speaker, lecturer, consultant, and author of *Life Unlocked: 7 Revolutionary Lessons to Overcome Fear*,[1] often speaks about the importance of possibility thinking and how it impacts our brains. Dr. Pillay, who is also CEO of NeuroBusiness Group, says that possibility thinking is what those of us who want to live an exceptional life must tap into. In fact, he says we are "wired for possibility." It's not about what's *probable*, because, as he states during one of his talks, "an exceptional life is a life of low probability."[2] If you get stuck thinking about what's *probable*, you will always limit yourself. Believing in the possibilities, Dr. Pillay says, allows us to put our imaginations to work.

As he writes in his *Debunking the Myths of the Mind* blog for *Psychology Today*: "No great discovery has ever been made when it was highly probable."[3] During those critical moments when you're making decisions about your life, your next career move, or your dreams, and others see "impossible," he advises that you ask yourself: If this were possible, what would I need to do? It's about what's *possible*; not what's probable.

We've talked in this book about letting go of the how and not trying to micromanage the ways support shows up for you or what it looks like. Instead, be aware of your reality, yes, but be *open* to possibility. I believe that support is what will help you close the gap between your reality and your possibility. You cannot just go on what you see, what the situation is right now, what the circumstances are, or which obstacles seem insurmountable at this time. Whether you're in a good situation or you're struggling in this moment, you have to believe in the possibility of something greater if you hope to continue to grow and evolve as a person. As I'm sure you've heard before in one way or another, if you are not growing or evolving, you are dying.

Another way to own your power and be open to the possibilities is to adopt the point of view that transformation coach Sylvia High suggested when I interviewed her on an early episode of my podcast, *Support is Sexy*.[4] Don't just believe in the possibility, know that you *are* a possibility, and know that you have been given the gift of choice. You are not a victim of your circumstances. You get to choose, you get to ask for support, you get to step into your possibility.

"Everything you do is a choice," Sylvia says during our interview. "Even choosing *not* to choose as a choice is paramount. You are the author of everything [so] be intentional. How you choose to relate to whatever life is serving you is critical. I think the other component is understanding that fundamentally, at the end of the day . . . you are a possibility. I believe God made us unlimited. Not that we do everything, but everything that we can create in the world is unlimited."

She continues, "I don't have all the gifts and talents, but whatever I want to create is available to me when I understand that I am a possibility and the rest of humanity is a possibility. So, understanding that you are a possibility given the gift of choice, when you combine those two together? *Whoa!* Whatever you want to do is available to you."

Sylvia says realizing that she is a possibility and that all that she wants to create and experience is within her also helps her have a sense of self-accountability. "When I wake up, after I give thanks for life, I say to God, 'Okay, God, what am I going to do with this possibility that I am today?'" she says. "And I tell you, when I'm slugging around, it doesn't feel comfortable. I'm like, 'Ooh, I'm wasting my possibility.'"

As women, we simply cannot afford to waste our possibility. And as we fight day in and day out for equal pay, gender equality, racial equality, our own human rights, and so much more around the world, I believe it's so important, especially now, that we believe in our possibility—individually, yes, and certainly collectively. Because when we do, we are unstoppable.

I know we all have times when our faith is tested, when things are unfair, when we feel disappointed or even angry, but if you don't believe somewhere in your core in the possibilities, and if you question your possibility and your capabilities, you cripple your dreams, you cap your imagination, and you start to let those self-defeating thoughts consume you. You start to believe the negative chatter outside from other people who only dream based on what they see, and, more detrimentally, you start to accept the negative chatter in your own head. It's the chatter within our own heads that is usually the hardest to ignore, right?

In his book *Life Unlocked*, Dr. Pillay says that in order to reprogram our brains to focus more on what's possible and counter that negative chatter, especially during trying or uncertain times, we have to change our thoughts about perceiving something as "impossible" and instead make the choice to see it as "difficult." "You don't have to know how you'll make a change," he writes (let go of the how, remember?), "you just have to believe a change will happen." I tell you from personal experience that this tiny shift in thinking, done intentionally and consistently, can move mountains in your life. And history has taught us that powerful movements around the world that have made our lives better were started by individuals who believed in a more beautiful possibility for us all.

Adopt possibility thinking, view yourself *as* a possibility, let support help you bridge the gap between your reality and the possibilities, and watch those mountains start to move.

TAKE ACTION:
CREATE YOUR "I AM"
STATEMENTS OF POSSIBILITY

One of the ways that I ensure that I consistently tap into my own possibility is by making affirming statements in the present using "I AM," and connecting those statements to the woman I know I am becoming. This is the woman I aspire to be. Not anyone or anything outside of myself. This woman, and her possibility, already exists within me. I just have to grow into her as I evolve each day.

So, maybe I don't have the tools, resources, knowledge, or something else at this time, but my daily "I AM" statements, which I write down in my I AM Journal, help me get there. I created the I AM Journal in order to keep these precious affirmations housed in a beautiful book that I love to pick up and open each day. But you can use any notebook or journal that you have if you want to get started today.

Writing in your I AM Journal is a daily practice that helps you get centered and grounded in the amazing person you already are today, and it will help you get clear on the person you are becoming. When you start your day by writing "I AM" statements and affirmations, it's like you are wrapping yourself in self-love before walking out the door. And by utilizing this practice to visualize your evolution—the person you are becoming and courageously stepping into—you acknowledge that you are the cocreator of your life. You align with who you feel called to be, not who everyone else says you are "supposed" to be.

As a lifelong learner and a lover of personal development, I constantly heard teachers and mentors speak about the power of "I AM" statements and affirmations. To help those statements stick—because, as we've discussed in early chapters, studies show that most of us learn better and remember things when we write them down—I utilized one of my favorite mediums, journaling. I have been journaling consistently since I was sixteen (and if you count my Hello Kitty diary—I've been at this since I was at least ten). That's thirty years and counting. I love having a space where I can freely dream, express myself, and reflect without judgment or a need for perfection. I also have been creating vision boards for more than a decade—posting images and quotes that resonate with me and that reflect my vision for my future self.

I often tell my coaching clients or listeners of my podcast, *Support is Sexy*, that you have to ask yourself: *Who is the woman I have to become, to become the woman I want to be? And how do I become that woman today?* These are questions that I reflect on daily as I reread my "I AM" statements related to the woman I am becoming. (Of course, you can easily replace "woman" with "man," "person," or whatever word best identifies who you are.)

Your "I AM" statements are like a blueprint. They keep you on track and aligned with who you *say* you are becoming and help you adopt a possibility mindset. When you feel yourself out of alignment, whether through action or thought, it's time to recalibrate and course correct. For example, if *I AM a* New York Times *best-selling author of books that inspire and motivate millions of women around the world* (that's actually one of my "I AM" statements), I am out of alignment with who I am called to be if I procrastinate on writing my book and let fear of not being "good enough" stop me from releasing it to the world (that was actually one of my fears). To course correct, I have to become the woman who gets up every single day and has dedicated time to write and edit my book, and I have to believe that becoming a *New York Times* best-selling author and impacting the lives of millions of women is a part of my possibility. Then, of course, I have to both seek and be open to the support that the Universe sends my way in order to help me step into that possibility.

To be clear, this practice of writing "I AM" statements in your journal is not magic, but it can be *magical*. And nothing is likely to happen overnight—although some things might. In other words, be open to the practice, to the possibilities, and to the idea that you are the cocreator of your life. You and your mind have more power in the way you experience your life than you think. As you commit to writing in your I AM Journal each day, you will eventually start to become much more aware of opportunities that support your vision for yourself, moments when you get to step into the you that you are becoming with the blessing of the Universe. As Paulo Coelho suggests in his classic book, *The Alchemist*, the universe conspires to help you achieve success.[5]

19

Be a Possibility Partner

Whether you're a woman entrepreneur who's running your own business or you're a leader within your organization who's managing your own department, creating a work environment where support is part of the company DNA can not only increase employee happiness and retention, it creates opportunity for possibility partnerships, where there's a give-and-take for all involved in helping one another excel. How many times have you heard an employee say that they're moving on from a company because they "just don't feel supported"? Or how often have you heard someone swear that they'll "never come back" on their way out the door? (How often have you actually been that person?)

This may not necessarily be because these people hated their job, their colleagues, or even their boss. This may be a result of an unintended closed-door policy that causes people to flee, one that cuts people off from having access to the kind of support they feel they need in the workplace—from simple delights to important factors related to their careers.

As the workforce shifts and considerations such as the desire for location-independent positions and flexible hours for employees present challenges for some companies and opportunities for others, business owners and executives are looking at new ways to incentivize great employees to come to their companies and convince their superstar employees to stay. If you are a leader in your organization, this creates an opportunity for you and your company to be a possibility partner for your employees and your teams, and to create space for support within your organization.

This is what Double Forte CEO Lee McEnany Caraher did in her business. Lee founded Double Forte—a San Francisco–based communications and public relations agency—in 2001, and she's proud to say that she has seen her share of employees come and go and come back again. And that's a good thing!

Lee, a baby boomer, focuses on supporting millennials in what she refers to as her once "senior-heavy" company. In fact, she hosted a podcast called *Millennial Minded*[1] that featured her and two of her millennial employees. On the podcast, Lee answered listener questions sent in to her cohosts and shared her expertise and career advice with them as a seasoned professional in her field.

But being "millennial minded," as Lee calls it, was not always the protocol at Double Forte. As she told me during our interview for the *Support is Sexy* podcast, she used to only recruit and hire individuals with at least ten years of experience, which meant most of the staff were Gen Xers or older. In 2009, though, after reevaluating the company's business model following the global financial crisis, Lee realized that there were going to be very few people with ten-plus years of experience in San Francisco, where she's based, so she began hiring for entry level positions again, which included more millennials. At the time, she thought this was great for business because she figured it would be cheaper to hire the less-seasoned candidates and also easier to grow her staff.

The result? Lee told me frankly during our interview: "I failed miserably. We had 100 percent failure rate with retaining millennials. . . . In one two-and-a-half month period, I lost every single millennial we hired. One person could have been their problem; but all of them? That had to be us."[2]

Lee started doing her own research to learn more about millennials overall, and found mostly negative information about what some consider the generation's sense of entitlement and flightiness when it comes to career. She decided to ignore it all and figure out a solution for her company and, later, for her clients, whose businesses were struggling in the same way. In fact, she began consulting clients on retaining their millennial employees and wrote her first book on the topic, *Millennials & Management: The Essential Guide to Making It Work at Work*.[3] Lee realized through her research that most CEOs were not offering guidance, training, and support for millennials on ways they can be successful in their first, second, and third jobs.

This new insight motivated Lee to take a new approach to how she and Double Forte supported their millennial employees, and it was a key turning point for her company as employees began to stay much longer.

The company's new strategy for support was to:

1. Always provide context first. Lee said when she started her own career, she did things because she was told to. But she found that millennials, who are known to be largely

mission-driven, care about "the why" when it comes to their work, so she provides them with that information rather than saying, "Because I'm the boss, and I said so."

2. Always ask for input on whatever you're creating so millennials (and anyone on your staff) may chime in with their insight from their unique perspective. You never know where a great idea is going to originate.

3. Have high expectations and say them out loud. Let your employees and colleagues know the measure of success so they have definitive goals. Also, provide support so others can reach those expectations and understand what achievement means.

Lee not only discovered that supporting her employees in this way—millennial or not—helped her company retain them, she found that when employees did leave to go work somewhere else, they were more likely to come back at some point. It is what Lee calls "the Boomerang Principle," which is also the title of her second book, *The Boomerang Principle: Inspire Lifetime Loyalty from Your Employees.*[4]

Lee believes that companies and organizations that allow and encourage former employees to return have a strategic advantage over those that don't. At Double Forte, a company of about thirty-five people, she says over the decade and a half that they have been in business, they have "rehired twelve or thirteen people once and rehired five people twice."

She suggests that business owners and bosses shift their mindset around the way they support and encourage employees who leave and want to come back, and she cringed when hearing her business colleagues say that if someone left their company, "They're dead to me." The sentiment from CEOs she spoke to was that they were resistant to wanting to pay to train their employees for fear that the employees might leave. But this lack of training—and a resistance to being a possibility partner for their staff—often ensured that employees left.

Instead, Lee advises that companies offer support to their employees by investing in them beyond salary with incentives like training, courses, and personal development that helps them advance professionally and personally, while still knowing that, yes, those people might just move on.

"It is hubris to think that a company can hold a person for their whole career," Lee says, especially since, if someone enters the workforce at age twenty-two or twenty-three today, they are likely going to have a sixty-year career.

When Lee brings a new person into her company, she tells them, "I know you're gonna leave me, and I hope you plan on coming back here."

She continues, "That is a sign of a great company, when great people come back to you. They go out into the world, they achieve something else for their own career goals that you cannot accommodate, and then, when you have moved forward, [your company] has moved forward, and that person has moved forward, there's an opportunity. Why would you not bring someone back who is the perfect hire, just because they left you the first time? As long as they left well, as long as you had a good experience with them, and as long as they can contribute, bring 'em back! Someone who returns to you is more valuable when they return to you than the day they left you, always."

Lee also believes the better you train people, the more you expose them to new opportunities and possibilities, the more likely they are to stick with your company longer because they want to stay and learn as much as they can. And, she says, every time you prolong someone's employment, keeping that person from leaving your company for at least a year, you save $100,000—which is considerable for any business, but especially for small businesses. And for Lee, the company's new point of view on supporting its employees through training and encouragement shortened her recruiting cycle by half. So, essentially, support is good for business.

Carrie Kerpen, CEO of the digital agency Likeable Media and author of *Work It: Secrets for Success from the Boldest Women in Business*, experienced the same success when she created a policy centered around support for her employees. In addition to being named a Top 50 Ad Agency and Top 50 Fastest-Growing Women-Owned Businesses by WPO and American Express OPEN, Likeable Media was voted by *Crain's* business magazine as one of the "Best Places to Work." For Carrie, employee happiness and productivity have always been priorities.[5]

Likeable was founded in 2006—just one year before Facebook opened to the public, expanding what would become its massive reach beyond Ivy League campuses, and made "social media" a part of our culture. Likeable was one of the first agencies to wisely move into the social media market, which gave it a major advantage. As the company continued to grow quickly, and Carrie took over as CEO from her husband/cofounder in 2013, she says she shifted Likeable from being a growth company focused on acquisition to focusing, instead, on 1) being profitable and 2) having a company that reflected her own vision as CEO, which included an emphasis on values and support.

During our interview for the *Support is Sexy* podcast, Carrie told me that one of the ways that she thinks the company is so, pun intended, likeable, is because it set core values, listened to what employees want, and made sure it supported them.

She admitted that the company couldn't do everything the employees requested (like "furball Fridays," when employees bring their pets to the office every Friday), but they could find ways to accommodate most requests (like one day when everyone brings in their pets for a companywide, pets-included photo shoot). Carrie says it's important to give employees real perks, as well as a sense of purpose and to let them know that they're supported and that their happiness is a company priority. [6]

When I catch up with Carrie a year after our first chat to interview her for this book, I ask her to tell me more about how she went about making employee happiness and a sense of support part of the culture at Likeable.

"Well, you know, I think agency culture in general is notoriously rough, [with] really rough hours, and it can be hard with work-life balance," she says, acknowledging the sometimes grueling nature of her industry. Carrie notes that this can be especially difficult for women in the industry. "[Reports] show that over 20 percent of mothers leave creative agencies after they've given birth because it's just not sustainable," she says. "For me, I was always driven by our mission to create a more likeable world, and I believe that that is a very important part of the culture that we create. I really wanted to be an agency that doesn't act like an agency, that gives our employees flex-time when needed and that supports them as they're going through some of the most challenging times of their lives. My long-term goal is to employ thousands of happy employees."

Oddly enough, some of Likeable's policies were so good to employees that some felt guilty for taking full advantage of them. For example, unlimited vacation time, which Carrie says the company has always offered, was just too much for some to handle. "It's funny, we just recently took unlimited vacation time, unlimited PTO [paid time off], and made it minimum PTO because [with] unlimited, people have trouble taking it because they feel guilty. When you don't have limits, you feel like you're always abusing it. So more recently we have put a minimum mandated [policy] that people have to take time off." Carrie said they also have flex hours for parents, where many of them work four day weeks and some work from home.

Now, of course, as a business that cares about employee happiness, you also have to care about employee performance. And Carrie says she and her team can see evidence of the positive impact it's having.

"I think employees know when you care," she says. "I think it has to be authentic. And when you have an organization that cares, it starts from the top and then goes to the leaders and then the director, then to management. You have to be able to truly show that you care about people and care about creating a workplace that matters and that you value employees first. I think that is what's key."

But this support and focus on happiness goes both ways. For Carrie, it wasn't just about seeing her employees happy. A large part of her focus is also on being a "happy, healthy CEO," something she often writes about when she contributes to outlets such as *Forbes* and *Inc.* When I ask her what makes her a happy CEO, Carrie says it's the possibility that she offers her employees that fulfills her. She says: "Nothing makes me happier than my ability to give back to the world, to be able to create jobs that [employees] will truly enjoy. I mean, that will be part of my legacy. The legacy that I leave on this earth will be that I gave a lot of people great careers, and I gave them an opportunity to grow."

When it comes to being a *healthy* CEO, Carrie, a woman after my own heart, says it's all about support. "I think you need a well-rounded support system. In my own book [*Work It: Secrets for Success from the Boldest Women in Business*], I talk about having a 'Fab PAB,' a fabulous personal advisory board. People that you can trust that are aligned with your vision. I think that's a very important thing that's in your life—personal or your business. And then always make sure that you take care of yourself," she continues. "Like that analogy about when you're with a kid on the airplane: put your life mask on first, and then put the mask on your child. Prioritize. Just think about yourself first, which is unnatural for most women. But you have to."

TAKE ACTION:
BE A (MINI) PARTNER IN POSSIBILITY

Maybe you don't have a company or a department to run just yet. Maybe, on an individual level, you don't have time to be a full-time mentor for someone right now. Maybe you can't take up every request to go for coffee. It's not that you don't want to, it's likely you've already overextended yourself and have enough to do, you ambitious woman you! So, how can you be someone's partner in possibility, even if for a moment, without overwhelming yourself, and without overextending yourself?

Be a mini partner. Take small steps. The reason I encourage you to take this approach personally is because these moments of possibility that you offer to other people on an individual level can inspire you just as much, give you a burst of energy, create new opportunities for you, and—at least—increase your good karma.

But, again, it doesn't have to be overwhelming. Here are a few simple ideas for how to be someone's partner in possibility (in small doses):

1. Send a colleague, contact, or friend a link to an article or post that you think might be interesting to them with a quick note that just says:

> Hi there,
> Saw this and thought you might find it interesting. Hope it's helpful! No need to respond. [And then add the link to the article or post you're sharing.]

I love to do this often on LinkedIn, where the context is clear that this is a professional outreach, if the person isn't a close friend or an acquaintance.

2. While standing in line waiting for your latte at the cafe, scroll through your text messages (instead of Instagram or Facebook) and look for a text from a colleague or contact you haven't spoken to in a while. Maybe it's someone you don't know well but you'd like to stay in touch with professionally. Perhaps you both spoke on a panel together, or you met at a conference and exchanged a few messages. Offer a bit of possibility. Send a quick text message that says:

> Hi there, it's [your first name and last name]. We met at [fill in the blank event or occasion]. Just reaching out to say it was great to meet you. When you get a chance, please let me know what's new with you. Would love to support, if I can. No rush to respond!

"Would love to support, **if I can**" tempers any expectation that, if that person has something big going on and needs support, you won't be expected to solve all his or her problems via text message.

"No rush to respond!" takes the pressure off your contact to feel forced to get back to you in that moment (or at all). Either way, you've made the outreach and offered the possibility for connection.

This outreach strategy of texting while in line at the cafe or during other periods of idle wait time (other than driving, of course) is a variation of one that I heard communications and social dynamics expert Jordan Harbinger share on *The James Altucher Show* podcast,[7] and I think it's brilliant. Not only do you reconnect and offer someone a bit of possibility, but you create space for your own possibility as well—all while being productive and using your idle time wisely. Jordan says this quick outreach can sometimes lead to someone offering you an opportunity such as a speaking engagement or something else that may support you. Even if something comes up later, thanks to your good vibes, you've likely been placed back at the top of that person's mental inbox. Give this strategy a try. I have done it several times, and it works. One of my possibility offers ended up with a hosting opportunity for me for an upcoming event the individual was planning at the time.

Again, don't worry that the person is going to write back with a huge ask. Most times, they shoot back a cordial response and simply say, "thank you for reaching out." That said, this might not be a tactic you want to use to reach out to a former intern or mentee. I think this somewhat personal outreach is a strategy best reserved for peers within your sphere of influence.

Speaking of mentees, if you're like me, you probably get regular requests to be a mentor—and you probably want to fulfill most of them because you're a good person who wants to help all the people all the time, obviously. But you simply cannot. There's only so much time. So, keep it simple. If someone asks if you can mentor him or her and you don't have the time (or maybe you're actually not interested), but you want to offer some possibility, you can offer feedback on one thing that he or she can do better. This doesn't imply that they're doing something "wrong," but we can all use feedback on how to possibly do something better. Remember, this is a smart twist on feedback that I received during my interview with Lisa Sun, CEO of Gravitas, who was mentioned in Chapter 14. Lisa says this is the way that she offers feedback now: by giving feedback on that one thing. (And, she suggests that this is a great way to request feedback as well. It makes it easier for the person whose insight you're requesting to focus and to respond without feeling overwhelmed.) Through your focused feedback—which should not suck you into a long back-and-forth, but should instead be brief marching orders for the recipient—you offer a bit of possibility.

20

Give Responsibly

When it comes to giving support, you might be thinking, "I got that covered!" After all, the primary reason for me writing this book is to remind you, the Queen of Giving, that you must remember to ask for support for yourself in the midst of all that generosity you got going on over there.

I know that you're going to continue to give, it's who you are, and I celebrate you for that. And to be clear, I don't want you to stop giving and only ask for support. But I do want you to give your support responsibly. Giving responsibly is another act of self-care and supporting yourself.

As a giver, you have to be willing to diligently guard not only your resources and your time, you have to guard your energy. Givers have to be aware of takers, no matter if you call them on their taking or you just envision the imaginary "taker" sign flashing in red on their foreheads as

187

you see their lips flapping and they ask you, yet again, for something. Takers can sense the lack of boundaries around you. It's on you to establish your own boundaries firmly and make sure those boundaries are clearly communicated.

Yes, support is sexy, but you're not stupid. And, more than that, you don't want your offers of support to make you sick. If you give and give until you're empty—from your bank account or your proverbial "cup"— you will be left depleted while the taker moves on to the next one.

Recognize the difference between offering support and being sucked dry. Know that you have a right to say: "No." And that "No" is a full sentence. You do not have to explain, and you do not have to say it apologetically. Just, No. The taker may be upset, but if he or she can't understand that you have a right to say no, and that there are going to be times when you *have* to say no, then: giver beware.

You can, if you choose, offer support. But having boundaries around that support is healthy, not selfish. So, don't feel guilty for putting some parameters in place. For example, you might say, "I can't do this other thing that you've asked; but here's what I can do." This is a generous way of saying: "This is it. Take it or leave it."

During an interview with Oprah Winfrey, best-selling author and spiritual teacher Iyanla Vanzant was asked if putting yourself first is selfish: "No, it's self-full," Iyanla says. "It's self-full to be first, to take care of you." She goes on to say that you have to be conscious of keeping your cup full, so to speak, referencing the phrase in Psalm 23 of the Bible, "My cup runneth over." What's in the cup is for you, the overflow is for others. This is how you create healthy boundaries.[1]

During that talk, Ms. Vanzant also references *A Course in Miracles*—created by Helen Schucman and William Thetford—and says that when you give and give and make a martyr of yourself, you make the other person a "thief." Because that individual is now stealing from you—your resources, your time, your joy, your peace—"and they don't even know it."[2]

Don't make other people in your life out to be thieves.

And don't sacrifice yourself as though you're destined to be the martyr.

Because, yes, there are takers out there, but you must also be honest with yourself about your own motivation. The pendulum of responsibility swings the other way as well. Are you giving because you really want to support this person, or are you desperately looking for some praise?

One way to know if your offer of support isn't from an authentic place—whether you're conscious of it or not—is if you're a person who gives, but you keep score. In this case, your action isn't about helping, it's about adding up the tally so you can either ask the recipient for all of it in return someday or you take joy in holding it over their heads for however long. This is not giving responsibly. This is being manipulative.

If you have some insecurity around why you're giving, you need to pause, examine the true reason, and unravel that.

Strive to have a genuine relationship with support and giving in the spirit of collaboration. There may be times when you give more, there may be times when the other person gives more; but when you know that you're giving honestly and responsibly, you can feel good about it either way.

You might have heard people quote a popular passage from the Bible that says, "God loves a cheerful giver." The full verse, taken from 2 Corinthians, chapter 9 verse 7, says: "Each one must give as he has decided in his heart, not reluctantly or under compulsion, for God loves a cheerful giver."

Give from your heart, but don't do so reluctantly or under compulsion. Your offer of support should bring you, and the recipient, joy.

TAKE ACTION:
SAY NO, AND MEAN IT

Practice embracing your "No." It doesn't have to be mean-spirited. But you should mean it. You are not obligated to say yes to every request. And you support yourself by being able to call upon your "No" to help you stick to your boundaries. Here are three times that you should know what it means to say, "No."

1. To people. It may be painful or uncomfortable, but the temporary discomfort for you and possible disappointment for the person making the request are worth it, considering that saying "yes" when you don't really have the time, energy, or expertise to support may waste even more time, resources, and energy for you both. You are being of service to yourself and to the other person even more by being honest. If you want or need to say "no," then do so.

2. To jobs, opportunities, work, and experiences that don't support you. When you say "yes" to something that you don't really want to do out of obligation or guilt or any other reason other than your pure enthusiasm about doing this thing or your love for this person, remember you are saying "no" to many other things that you may actually want to do. Every "yes" over here means "no, no, no, and no" over there.

3. To things you may actually *want* to do. You may have to embrace your "no" even when you do want to have an experience, take advantage of an opportunity, or support someone. But sometimes "no" is necessary to allow you to focus on what matters in the moment. Perhaps you have a deadline, perhaps there's a goal that you really want to reach. The FOMO of your "no" for you in the short term is a small price to pay if it may pay major dividends later.

I can't tell you how many times I have winced saying "no" to opportunities or experiences or fun times with friends while I have been writing this very book and experienced FOMO (fear of missing out). Trips, parties, events, get-togethers, even occasional excursions while I was on my trip to different countries with Remote Year—I had to turn down many. But I knew that a "yes" to those invitations for a temporary good time—no matter how amazing I knew it was going to be—meant a "no" to me being able to focus on delivering my best work and completing this great feat of writing my very first book. There were already moments when it was difficult enough to write because of all the noise—in my head and in the world that we live in. Learning how to embrace "no" helped me create space for my dream, allowed me to focus, and, ultimately, enabled me to be of service to hopefully support you and millions of others in a bigger, less selfish way through this work.

21

Know That It's Bigger Than You

One of the most powerful lessons I learned when I attended that transformational Momentum Education workshop in New York in 2015 (see the Introduction) is not just about how much asking for support serves me, which it certainly does, but also how much asking for support for myself and my dreams also serves the world.

When you *don't* ask for support for your goals and dreams, you're actually being selfish. (I know, I never thought of it this way either.) Sometimes we may be led to think that asking for support is what makes us selfish. It's the opposite. When you don't ask for support, you're denying the world your greatest gifts, your highest good, the possibility of your highest contribution. Especially since, let's be real, up until now, it's likely that the reason that you're not asking for support has more to do with your ego or your desire to save face or a story you're telling yourself about what negative implication asking for support has on you and your reputation than it does your concern that you might inconvenience someone. Am I right?

But, how dare you? How dare you deny the world of your gifts? How dare you not live up to your highest potential? This doesn't mean doing the most for the sake of doing the most. Or that you're taking on all the responsibilities. And it does not necessarily mean doing more than you're doing right now. But I believe it does mean being honest with yourself and thinking about ways that you can get support for the things in your life that fulfill you and that make you happy and that help you be more motivated to help others be fulfilled in their lives as well—whether that's through your work or in your personal life.

In other words: it's bigger than you, sis. This isn't just about your own success, because we are all connected, more than many of us realize.

To quote part of one of my favorite passages from author and spiritual teacher Marianne Williamson's powerful book *A Return to Love: Reflections on the Principles of A Course in Miracles*: "You are a child of God. Your playing small doesn't serve the world. There's nothing enlightened about shrinking so that other people won't feel insecure around you. We are all meant to shine, as children do. We were born to make manifest the glory of God that is within us. It's not just in some of us; it's in everyone. And as we let our own light shine, we unconsciously give other people permission to do the same. As we're liberated from our own fear, our presence automatically liberates others."[1]

THINK FOR A MOMENT

What would the world be like if you truly stepped into your greatness and let your light shine?

How would having support light you up in new ways you may never have imagined?

What impact might this new light within you have on your family, your community, your company, your business, and beyond?

When I think about how this mindset shift has helped me stop playing small, I think about all the ways that I have had to work hard to stop hiding, especially in my business. As an online entrepreneur and podcast host, it's easy to stay tucked away behind my computer or behind the microphone and pretend that I'm playing full out. But really, I had been using both as a mask to help me keep hiding. It's not that I didn't want to be fully present in my business, it's that I had to be honest with myself that I was allowing my ego to get the best of me, hold me back, and make me continue to play smaller than I know I'm capable of. (I know I talk about the importance of taking imperfect action, but I never said it was easy!) So when I'm doing something new—whether that's launching my own television show featuring inspiring women of color entrepreneurs or hopping on Facebook Live to chat directly with my community—I have to force myself to get out there, even if it's imperfect.

Not raggedy, because nobody wants that, right? But imperfect, knowing that, with support—and plenty of practice—it will get better with each try. Because how can you improve on something if you haven't yet created anything to improve upon and you haven't given it a try? You cannot get better if you do not get started.

If it were the case that I didn't want to do any of these things, or I didn't think they'd be of tremendous service to my audience or community, then there would be no reason to give it a second thought. But I believe the opposite. I know that appearing in videos and showing up more in person—virtually, on television, and at meetups I've begun to host—helps me connect to the women I hope to reach in a new and even more intimate way. By choosing to play small and continuing to hide, I'd be focusing on myself and my ego and not focusing on my audience, people who have expressed interest in learning from me or getting to know what I have to offer. So, what I choose to do is to get support with breaking through those fears and unraveling my own limiting beliefs, whether that's through courses I take or through mastermind groups I belong to or through private sessions with my coach, who holds me accountable for stepping courageously outside my comfort zone. By the time this book is released, God willing, you'll see my smiling face everywhere, so prepare yourself!

In what ways are you hiding or playing small? In what healthy ways could you be of service to the world if you stopped holding back or being held hostage by your ego? In what ways could getting support help you play full out so you can show up as your best self? How will getting over "I got it!" help free you from trying to do it all on your own?

Remember, it's bigger than you. And having support matters to us all as women now more than ever.

This is about putting ourselves in positions where we can help one another, within our communities, within our work, and around the world. As each of us rises, we can pull another woman up to her next level. As one woman moves forward, makes a breakthrough, cracks the glass ceiling, we all gain the inspiration to dream bigger. As you begin to own your power and use your voice, you are better able to create space for other women whose voices aren't often heard. As you bravely step into those rooms that may be difficult to get into, you have the opportunity to hold the door and create a seat at the table for the next woman. Having support helps those important moments happen more often than when we struggle to do it all on our own.

I acknowledge that, for some, support may seem like a privilege—and perhaps our society has it set up this way, especially in certain parts of the world where women are oppressed in ways that deny them access to education, blocking their rights to make decisions about their own well-being, and, in the worst cases, inflicting violence on them when they advocate for themselves. Even in the United States, we have to acknowledge that support for certain segments of the population is prioritized over support for others based unfairly on factors such as race, socioeconomic realities, gender, and more. So, support may not be as readily available for everyone as I believe it should be. But it doesn't have to be this way. If we all understand that each of us deserves support, and we are committed to making sure that none of us feels alone, isolated, or without the support we need, no matter where we are in the world, we have the power to make change. If we speak up for one another and use our voices to support one another, whether near or far, we create a vision of new possibilities for our sisters in our communities and around the world who may be struggling, or who may just need that opened door.

So, as we, as unapologetically ambitious women, continue to move into more powerful positions of leadership in all industries, redefine what success is for each of us, and create lives we love, let's remember how important it is to support one another and to ask for support for ourselves. This doesn't mean that we all agree with one another; but there is an opportunity for us to understand, connect, and have compassion for one another.

Get over "I Got It!" Syndrome, and let's get busy embracing one another and saving this world. Together.

ENDNOTES

Introduction

1. Vanessa Friedman, "Andy Spade's Statement about Kate Spade's Death," June 6, 2018, *New York Times*, https://www.nytimes.com/2018/06/06 /style/andy-spade-statement.html.
2. Holly Hedegaard, MD, Sally C. Curtin, MA, and Margaret Warner, PhD, "Suicide Rates in the United States Continue to Increase," NCHS Data Brief, No. 309, June 2018, https://www.cdc.gov/nchs/data/databriefs /db309.pdf.
3. Dr. Srinivasan Pillay, "Why Focusing on Your Goals Will Make You Poor," May 17, 2017, Medium, https://medium.com/@drsrini/why-focusing-on -your-goals-will-make-you-poor-4928e9339683, and on his website, https://drsrinipillay.com/, where he discusses possibility thinking.

Chapter 2

1. Maggie Minor, *Support is Sexy* podcast with Elayne Fluker, episode 310, September 20, 2017, http://elaynefluker.com/podcast/maggie-minor.
2. Katherine C. Nordal, PhD, quoted in American Psychological Association (2017), *Stress in America: Coping with Change*. Stress in America™ Survey, p. 3, https://www.apa.org/news/press/releases/stress/2016/coping-with -change.pdf.
3. US Department of Health and Human Services, National Institute of Mental Health, NIH Publication No. 20-MH-4779, "Depression in Women: 5 Things You Should Know," https://www.nimh.nih.gov/health /publications/depression-in-women/index.shtml.
4. The World Health Organization, January 20, 2020, https://www.who.int /news-room/fact-sheets/detail/depression.

5. US Department of Health and Human Services, National Institute of Mental Health, NIH Publication No. 20-MH-4779, "Depression in Women: 5 Things You Should Know," https://www.nimh.nih.gov/health /publications/depression-in-women/index.shtml.

Chapter 4

1. Dr. Zoe Shaw, *Redefining Your Superwoman* podcast, https://drzoeshaw.com /podcast/.

Chapter 8

1. Kathryn Finney, "Closed Mouths Don't Get Fed: Black Women and the Language of the Ask," October 1, 2015, Medium, https://medium.com /@KathrynFinney/closed-mouths-don-t-get-fed-black-women-and-the -language-of-the-ask-da750ee4a9f8.
2. Kirsten Chuba, "Taraji P. Henson Opens Up about Seeking Mental Health Treatment," September 23, 2018, *Variety*, https://variety.com/2018/scene /news/taraji-p-henson-mental-health-foundation-1202953695/.
3. Dr. Brené Brown, "Listening to Shame," TED Talk, 2012, https://www.ted .com/talks/brene_brown_listening_to_shame#t-232086.

Chapter 9

1. Dr. Brené Brown, "Listening to Shame," TED Talk, 2012, https://www.ted .com/talks/brene_brown_listening_to_shame#t-232086.

Chapter 10

1. Lesley Jane Seymour, *Support is Sexy* podcast with Elayne Fluker, episode 663, July 3, 2019, http://elaynefluker.com/podcast/lesley-jane-seymour/.

Chapter 12

1. *The David Rubenstein Show*, March 1, 2017, https://www.youtube.com /watch?v=-4cCDo85_VA&feature=youtu.be.
2. Michelle Villalobos, *Support is Sexy* podcast with Elayne Fluker, episode 358, November 29, 2017, elaynefluker.com/podcast/michelle-villalobos/.

Chapter 14

1. Lisa Sun, *Support is Sexy* podcast with Elayne Fluker, episode 603, February 4, 2019, http://elaynefluker.com/podcast/lisa-sun/.

Chapter 15

1. Ava DuVernay, *The Van Jones Show*, March 11, 2018, https://www.youtube
.com/watch?v=xUimjFHfcps.
2. Dr. Gail Matthews, "Goals Research Summary," Dominican University of
California, https://www.dominican.edu/sites/default/files/2020-02/gail
matthews-harvard-goals-researchsummary.pdf.

Chapter 16

1. Mel Robbins, *The 5-Second Rule: Transform Your Life, Work and Confidence
with Everyday Courage* (New York: Savio Republic, 2017).

Chapter 17

1. Traci Baxley, "Social Justice Parenting," TEDx, https://tracibaxley.com
/social-justice-parenting/.

Section Four

1. Sylvia High, *Support is Sexy* podcast with Elayne Fluker, episode 44,
September 1, 2016, http://elaynefluker.com/podcast/sylvia-high/.

Chapter 18

1. Dr. Srinivasan S. Pillay, *Life Unlocked: 7 Revolutionary Lessons to Overcome
Fear* (Emmaus, PA: Rodale Books, 2011), https://www
.amazon.com/dp/1609611462.
2. Dr. Srinivasan S. Pillay, *Life More Abundant* podcast, hosted by Sean
Croxton, episode 284, https://seancroxton.com/quote-of-the-day/284/.
3. Dr. Srinivasan Pillay, "Living Life Fully: The Possibility Quotient (PQ),"
February 20, 2011, *Psychology Today*, https://www.psychologytoday.com/us/blog
/debunking-myths-the-mind/201102/living-life-fully-the-possibility-quotient-pq.
4. Sylvia High, *Support is Sexy* podcast with Elayne Fluker, episode 44,
September 1, 2016, http://elaynefluker.com/podcast/sylvia-high/.
5. Paulo Coelho, *The Alchemist* (New York: HarperOne, Original, 1993,
Anniversary Edition, 2014), https://www.amazon.com/Alchemist-Paulo
-Coelho/dp/0062315005.

Chapter 19

1. Lee McEnany Caraher, host, *Millennial Minded* podcast, http://millennial
mindedpodcast.com/.

2. Lee McEnany Caraher, *Support is Sexy* podcast with Elayne Fluker, episode 554, October 1, 2018, http://elaynefluker.com/podcast/lee-caraher/.

3. Lee McEnany Caraher, *Millennials & Management: The Essential Guide to Making It Work at Work* (United Kingdom: Routledge, 2014).

4. Lee McEnany Caraher, *The Boomerang Principle: Inspire Lifetime Loyalty from Your Employees* (United Kingdom: Routledge, 2017).

5. Carrie Kerpen, *Work It: Secrets for Success from the Boldest Women in Business* (New York: TarcherPerigee, 2018).

6. Carrie Kerpen, *Support is Sexy* podcast with Elayne Fluker, episode 218, May 8, 2017, http://elaynefluker.com/podcast/carrie-kerpen/.

7. Jordan Harbinger, *The James Altucher Show* podcast, episode 181, August 23, 2016, https://jamesaltucher.com/podcast/jordan-harbinger/.

Chapter 20

1. Iyanla Vanzant, *Oprah's Lifeclass*, March 28, 2012, https://www.youtube.com/watch?v=ZhqokZF5OFU.

2. Ibid.

Chapter 21

1. Marianne Williamson, *A Return to Love: Reflections on the Principles of a Course in Miracles* (New York: HarperCollins, 2009).

ACKNOWLEDGMENTS

To the people I love and those who love and support me. I hope I made you proud.

MOM & DAD: My heart, my heroes. Thank you for always believing in me, even if, sometimes, you thought I was crazy. I forgive you because you were probably right.

THE GIRLS: April McKoy Robinson, Laticha Brown, Erica Hines, Erin Riggins, Tia Bennett, Atiya Jackson, Nataki Edwards, and Tari Linnear. I could not do what I do or be who I am without you all in my world.

DOPEST CHEERLEADERS: Shahara Jackson, Tai Beauchamp, Erika Perry, and Taiia Smart Young. For being there for advice, feedback, and support, whether I needed you to cheer me on or to cheer me up.

COVER QUEENS: Kelly Notaras and Renata Dolz for helping me get over myself and choose the best cover for my book. :)

MY TRAVEL ROOMIE: Polina Hanin for being the first human to read an early draft of the book. I will never forget our chat about it over lunch at a cafe in Prague. I am grateful for your friendship.

MY SUPPORT IS SEXY SiSTERS: For every woman (and a few good men!) who listen to my podcast, who have been inspired to start a business by it, or who have continued on because of it, I hope you know I see you, I love you, and I appreciate you. It just would not be the same without you.

THE COACH: Margo Geller for knowing when to talk me down off the ledge and when to encourage me to make some noise. You are never getting rid of me! :)

THE WOMAN WITH VISION: Barbara Biziou for reminding me to be the star of my own show.

THE SPARK: Serial entrepreneur Jen Groover for saying, "I think you're onto something" about *Support is Sexy*. You were definitely right.

THE AGENT: Nick Chiles for believing in the vision and helping me stick with it. Also for keeping it real and putting up with my "but what about . . . ?" questions.

THE SUPPORT: Corynne Corbett for being a shining example of "Support is Sexy" and letting me know that Nick was now an agent.

THE LITERARY LOBBYIST: Book publicist Dawn Michelle Hardy for helping me get through this process with your incredible insight very early on and for putting this book out into the world as only you can.

THE MENTORS: Monique Greenwood, Rosemarie Robotham, Robin Stone, Claire McIntosh, Linda Villarosa, and Susan Taylor, who taught me how to tell a story—mine and those of the women I love to serve—with heart and purpose.

THE BRAVE: To each and every person who allowed me to interview you for this book. Thank you for saying yes and for trusting me with your story. You will forever be a part of this important chapter in my life.

SPECIAL THANK YOU TO BLACK WOMEN: You inspire me with your strength, grace, and resilience. You are unmatched and pure magic every single day. I pray you know that you DESERVE support. And you matter.

THE CREW: Photographer Mecca Gamble, image consultant Tamara Flemings, hairstylist Kanisha Gordon, makeup artist Tiana Brown, videographer Diamonde Williamson, and the video production team led by Adrienne Nicole. Thank you for making me feel like my most beautiful and pulled-together self for this very special moment.

MY A-TEAM: Courtney Daniel and Sarah Tulloch—your support is beyond. Now let's get this coin!

THE EDITORS: To the HarperCollins Leadership team. We did it! Thank you.

INDEX

INDEX

ABOUT THE AUTHOR

Elayne Fluker is host of the *Support is Sexy* podcast, which has more than eight hundred thousand downloads and features her interviews with more than five hundred diverse and inspiring women entrepreneurs. Elayne is also the Founder of SiS.Academy—an online learning platform educating and empowering Black women entrepreneurs. In 2020, she was named a "Founder of Change" for SiS.Academy as part of the American Express "100 for 100" program featuring one hundred innovative Black women entrepreneurs. As a trusted coach and consultant for high-potential women around the world, Elayne helps her clients shift their mindset around support so they can move to their next level. She has led more than two hundred workshops globally in Spain, Morocco, South Africa, and the United States. She has shared her expertise at LinkedIn, Hewlett-Packard, New York University, Columbia University, Howard University, Spelman College, and the United Nations. She has appeared on CNN, the *TODAY* show, *Nightline*, *Inside Edition*, *Extra*, BET, HLN, Satellite XM Radio, and many others, and she has appeared as a guest on more than twenty-four podcasts, sharing her message of support for women.